31

DEVOTIONALS

Vol.1

Jeremy Baker

31 Devotionals, Vol.1

Some illustrations are from personal experience. All other illustrations and quotes have been cited in the appendix unless are hearsay or unknown.

Printed in the United States of America

First Printing, June 2018

ISBN 978-1-7323830-0-5

www.thenxtgeneration.com

CONTENTS

CONTENTS

INTRODUCTION

This is a 31 day devotional that will help inspire, motivate, and encourage you to grow deeper in your relationship with God. It is vitally important to seek out practical habits that will cause intentional growth each and every day.

We live in a society where average is acceptable, but those who are willing to take the challenge and develop themselves will have greater levels of success in life. Growth does not happen by accident; growth is caused by intention and action. The choices you make today impact your tomorrow. Where are you now? Where do you want to be in the future? How do you achieve the dreams and goals in your heart?

The best action we can take today is to grow ourselves so we are empowered to face tomorrow. The Lord is a rewarder of those who seek Him daily. It is known that it takes 30 days to form a habit. I believe as you take the next 31 days to purposely commit yourself to set time aside to go through this book, you will grow and be challenged to go to your next level. Make it a point to have your heart open to receive from the Lord and be willing to do whatever it takes to be all God has called you to be. You can take the stairs, or you can take the elevator. The choice is in your hands.

Jeremy Baker

1

HOPE

DAY 1

HOPE

//BIG THOUGHT//

Never lose hope! You never know what tomorrow may bring.

STORY >>> Baby Jessica

"October 14th, 1987, little 18 month old Jessica was playing in her aunt's backyard in Midland, TX. As she was walking, she fell into a well that was 8 inches in diameter, and 22 feet into the ground. She was trapped in that well for 58 hours! People from all over the country came to her rescue, from engineers and firefighters to professional drillers. They had a passion to help all because they believed in saving this little girl's life. The amazing thing about this story is that everyone, no matter who they were, or what walk of life they came from, was filled with hope that they were going to save her life - and they did! A miracle happened because they chose to live in HOPE!"[1]

Hope is simply believing and trusting that no matter what's going on in your life, God always has a plan. Hope is knowing that He will never leave you alone. Hope is being completely sure that God is a GOOD God who cares for YOU.

Today you might be in a well of problems, trouble or conflict; but God is with you. He will never leave you. He knows everything about you. He made you. He will give you hope as you trust in Him!

//LET'S READ//

Hebrews 10:23 (ESV) -

Let us hold fast the confession of our hope without wavering, for He who promised is faithful.

Romans 15:13 (ESV) -

May the God of hope fill you with all joy and peace in believing, so that by the power of the Holy Spirit you may abound in hope.

Look at this verse! It says - The God of HOPE!

Not the god of doubt!
Not the god of fear!
Not the god of stress!
Not the god of anxiety!
Not the god of worry!
Not the god of hopelessness!
But He is the God of Hope!

BE ENCOURAGED! YOU SERVE A GOD OF HOPE!!

STORY >>> The Paralyzed Man

"In Mark 2, we find the story of a man who was paralyzed. This man had four incredible friends who wanted to bring him to Jesus. As they picked him up, they took him through the city to where Jesus was. The place was so crowded that there was no room to get through any door, but hope is always stronger than fear. They decided not to give up. They climbed on top of the building, broke through the ceiling, and lowered the paralyzed man through the ceiling to Jesus. Let's take a look at what happens in verse 5 – And when Jesus saw their faith, He said to the paralytic, "Son, your sins are forgiven." According to the Bible, immediately, the paralyzed man, was now completely healed. I want to point something out to you. Jesus saw the friend's faith, He saw their hope. Hope is such a powerful thing. The man took up his mat and left praising God. The man found hope through Jesus. It looked like a hopeless situation, but Jesus was there! (Mark 2:1-12, ESV) Hope is an expectation that is crucial to have."

Let your hope in Jesus be unbreakable and unshakable. Do not stand on the problems of life or on bad circumstances, but stand on the great promises of the God of hope!

Romans 12:12 (ESV) -

Rejoice in hope, be patient in tribulation, be constant in prayer.

It says rejoicing in hope! Always rejoice in hope - NOTHING ELSE! If you can keep hope alive, it will keep you alive. Hope has power!

Psalm 62:5 (ESV) -

For God alone, O my soul, wait in silence, for my hope is from Him.

God brings us real hope. Hope that we can always count on. Today, be encouraged to make the God of Hope your hope! Through Christ, you can have a confident expectation that far exceeds any worldly hope.

THINK ON IT

1. What is hope?

___

___

___

___

2. What do you need hope in?

___

___

___

___

___

3. What can you do daily to make sure that God is the God of hope in your life?

"Once you choose hope anything is possible."
- Christopher Reeves

Notes

Notes

2

COMMITMENT

DAY 2

COMMITMENT

//BIG THOUGHT//
In order to go to your next level in life, it's going to take commitment.

> *"Most people fail, not because of lack of desire but, because of lack of commitment."*
> – Vince Lombardi [2]

Commitment: *An agreement or pledge to do something.*

Unless a commitment is made, there are only promises and hopes; but no plans. I've always heard that a dream without a goal is a wish. The Bible says in Proverbs 16:3 (ESV), "Commit your work to the Lord, and your plans will be established."

Have you ever played the game called "Hokey Pokey"? It's the little kid's game where you sing, dance and follow the instructions. You know, you put your left hand in and your left hand out; your right hand in and your right hand out, and you shake it all about, and then you "turn yourself around." My favorite part is when you put your whole self in...

Romans 12:1 (ESV) -
I appeal to you therefore, brothers, by the mercies of God, to present your bodies as a living sacrifice, holy and acceptable to God, which is your spiritual worship.

To be a "living sacrifice" means to commit your whole self in. Just like the "Hokey Pokey". This is what Paul is talking about in this passage of scripture. He's saying to be totally committed. If you have this kind of commitment, you will go to the next level, guaranteed.

When it comes to commitment, there are 4 different types of people:

1. **Cop-out:** An individual who avoids doing what they know they have to do (procrastination)
2. **Hold-out:** An individual who is wanting to accomplish something, but just keeps making excuses
3. **Drop-out:** An individual who begins something, but quits before it is finished
4. **All-out:** An individual who is committed and willing to do whatever it takes to go all the way

A person who desires to be an all-out, has a mindset that says to himself/herself >>

I'm committed >>
To my family
To my church
To my friends
To my work
To my calling
To my dreams
To see God move in my life

2 Chronicles 16:9 (ESV) -

The eyes of the Lord ranges throughout the earth to strengthen those whose hearts are fully committed to Him.

This verse makes me think of this story about Julius Caesar.

> *"When Julius Caesar landed on the shores of Britain with his Roman legions, he took a bold and decisive step to ensure the success of his military venture. Ordering his men to march to the edge of the Cliffs of Dover, he commanded them to look down at the water below. To their amazement, they saw every ship in which they had crossed the channel engulfed in flames. Caesar had deliberately cut off any possibility of retreat. Now that his soldiers were unable to return to the continent, there was nothing left for them to do but to advance and conquer! And that is exactly what they did."*[3]

Talk about commitment! Once he did that, there was no going back. That is the kind of attitude of the heart that you must have in order to fulfill your destiny. Some people want everything to be perfect before they're willing to commit, but commitment always precedes achievement. When you make a commitment, you create hope. When you keep a commitment, you create trust!

//LET'S READ//

Matthew 6:24 (ESV) -
"No one can serve two masters, for either he will hate the one and love the other, or he will be devoted to the one and despise the other. You cannot serve God and money."

Proverbs 4:23 (ESV) -
Keep your heart with all vigilance, for from it flow the springs of life.

Mark 8:36 (ESV) -
For what does it profit a man to gain the whole world and forfeit his soul?

My commitment **reveals my value.** **(Matthew 6:24)**
My commitment **shapes my life.** **(Proverbs 4:23)**
My commitment **determines my destiny.** **(Mark 8:36)**

ONE FINAL THOUGHT:
If you choose to leave the chair of commitment you will always have to compromise, which leads to conflict.

THINK ON IT:

1. Commitment always starts on the inside (heart). You have to choose to be committed in all your ways!

2. Commitment is more than just words; it's action. Faith is not passive, but faith is active.

3. Commitment opens great opportunities. When you are faithful and committed to what you are doing, God will open up new opportunities.

Notes

Notes

3

DREAM BIG

DAY 3

DREAM BIG

//BIG THOUGHT//

Our destiny is determined by the number of times that we get up, dust ourselves off, and chase our dreams.

Proverbs 16:3 (ESV) -

Commit your work to the Lord, and your plans will be established.

Story//

> *"A young man dreamed of being an actor, but in the early 1980's, he wasn't getting the big parts he wanted. He had grown up so poor that his family lived in a Volkswagen van down by the ocean, struggling to just get by in life. Broke and discouraged, he drove his beat-up old car to the top of a hill overlooking the city of LA and did something unusual.*
>
> *He wrote himself a check for 10 million dollars for acting services rendered. He put that check in his wallet and kept it there.*
>
> *When things got tough, he'd pull out the check and look at it to remind himself of his dream.*
>
> *Through his hard work and commitment, a dozen years later, that same young man was making $16-$25 million dollars a movie. His name is Jim Carrey. No matter how hard life is, or how rough it gets, always have your dream before you so you can see where you're going."* [4]

Just as Jim Carrey kept the check in his wallet to remind himself of his dream, we should do the same. Whether it's the picture of your dream truck on the dashboard of your car. Or if it's a picture of your dream house in your apartment or a picture of your dream on the homescreen of your phone. Every day, see your dream and speak life over it and work towards it until it comes to pass.

A dream drives you to greatness.
Your dreams can come true.

The poorest person in the world isn't a person without money, it's a person without a dream.

It's time to chase your dreams.
God cares about your dreams.

God himself has a dream for your life that predates the birth of the stars, galaxies, and planets. **YOU ARE A BIG DEAL!** Don't let anyone tell you differently. God wants you to dream. He wants you to dream about the impossible becoming possible. That is who God is; He is the dream-maker!

I am not going to let others >>
Shut me up
Shut me down
Shut me out
Shut me in

Jeremiah 29:11 (ESV) -
For I know the plans I have for you, declares the Lord, plans for welfare and not for evil, to give you a future and a hope.

There will be those days that...
People will tell you NO
Friends will tell you NO
Family will tell you NO
Banks will tell you NO
Bosses will tell you NO
Industries will tell you NO

But God's Yes is bigger than their NO! Make up your mind, tell yourself you are not going to quit. NEVER! If you're looking for an excuse, you'll always find one. If you're looking for an opportunity, you'll always find one.

I'm dreaming BIG, because I serve a BIG God who has BIG plans for my life!

Psalm 37:4 (ESV) -

Delight yourself in the Lord, and he will give you the desires of your heart.

Be a Dream Chaser, because He's the Dream Maker. Sometimes, because of the things we have gone through in life, we need to tell our heart to dream again! Maybe life didn't turn out like you had hoped, or maybe you're just sitting on the sidelines of life, tired. It's time to tell your heart to dream again. Our incredible, majestic God breathed His life into you. You've got what it takes! This is your time, your moment! Shake off fear, insecurity, and doubt! It's time to dream and dream BIG, because greater is He that is in you than He that is in the world! **(1 John 4:4)**

THINK ON IT -

1. How big is your dream? (You serve a BIG God, so you should dream BIG!)

2. What are things you can do every day to visualize your dream?

3. What are dream stealers in your life?

Notes

Notes

4

FORWARD

DAY 4

FORWARD

//BIG THOUGHT//

God hasn't made you to go backwards, God has made you to go forward!

Sometimes the smallest step in the right direction ends up being the biggest step of your life.

> **Forward:** *Moving, tending, getting ready for the future.*[5]

Philippians 3:12-14 (ESV) -

Not that I have already obtained this or am already perfect, but I press on to make it my own, because Christ Jesus has made me his own. Brothers, I do not consider that I have made it my own. But one thing I do: forgetting what lies behind and straining forward to what lies ahead, I press on toward the goal for the prize of the upward call of God in Christ Jesus.

God has not called us to bunker down, but God has called us to take ground. The enemy always wants you to bunker down. The enemy has a plan for your life. He comes to kill, steal and destroy. **(John 10:10)** Jesus came to give us life right now. The kind of life He came to give us is a life of forward movement, a life that is always growing and flourishing.

STORY // Healing on the Sabbath

> "*Again, he entered the synagogue, and a man was there with a withered hand. And they watched Jesus, to see whether he would heal him on the Sabbath, so that they might accuse him. And He said*

> *to the man with the withered hand, "Come here." And He said to them, "Is it lawful on the Sabbath to do good or to do harm, to save life or to kill?" But they were silent. And He looked around at them with anger, grieved at their hardness of heart, and said to the man, "Stretch out your hand." He stretched it out, and his hand was restored.*"
> **(Mark 3:1-5, ESV)**

By this man stretching his hand forward, there was an instant healing that took place. <<**STEP FORWARD!**>>

> The moment you're ready to quit is usually the moment right before a miracle happens!

Turning back leaves you powerless to move forward!

STORY // The Australian Coat of Arms

> "*The Australian coat of arms has a picture of two creatures - the emu, a flightless bird, and the kangaroo. It is suspected that these two animals were chosen, because they share a characteristic that appealed to the Australian citizens. Both the emu and the kangaroo can move only forward, not backward! The emu's three-toed foot causes it to fall if it tries to go backwards. The kangaroo is prevented from moving in reverse because of its large tail!*"

Be focused on going forward in the game of life! Think about an army marching toward its enemy. They have orders from their leadership. They are marching forward and taking ground. They are doing what they are told to do.

Proverbs 4:25 says, *"Let your eyes look directly forward, and your gaze be straight before you."* What if the men started to look from side to side? They would become distracted. In order to move forward in life, you have to focus. Whatever you focus on, has your attention. Whatever has your attention, has your focus.

If you don't grow forward, you will always be in the same place!

CONFESSION:

- I am moving forward and not looking back.
- I am moving forward in every area of my life.
- The best days of my life are before me.
- God directs my steps.
- I am moving forward!

THINK ON IT

Nothing in your life is permanent, there is always a way to move forward.

1. What are the things that you know you need to move forward in?

____

____

____

____

____

2. What are some steps you can take to move forward?

____

____

____

____

____

5

MINDSET

MINDSET

//BIG THOUGHT//

Your mindset matters, it affects everything in your life.

It has been estimated that an average brain has anywhere from 25,000 to 50,000 thoughts a day, and 70% of them are believed to be negative.[6]

That's 50,000 x 365 = 18,250,000 thoughts per year!

If you think big, you go big in life.
If you think little, you go little in life.

It is time to control your thought process, to think big; because you serve a BIG God!

The God that can do the impossible; the miracle-working God; the God that is able not just sometimes, but ALL the time! It is so important that you have the right mindset as you go through life. The mindset you have of yourself, your circumstances, and your life, become your reality. There are times in life that can cause you to just start thinking crazy.

Story// The Elephant Mindset

"One day a man was passing by some elephants, he suddenly stopped, confused by the fact that these huge creatures were being held by only a rope tied to their legs. It was obvious that the elephants could, at anytime, break away from the ropes they were tied to, but for some reason, they did not. He saw a trainer nearby and asked why these beautiful, magnificent animals just stood there and made no attempt to get away.

"Well", the trainer said, "when they are very young and much smaller,

we use the same size rope to tie them up then as we do now, and it's enough to hold them. As they grow up, they are conditioned to believe they cannot break away. They believe the rope can still hold them, so they never try to break free." He was amazed. These animals could at any time break free from their bonds but because they believed they couldn't, they were stuck right where they were. This powerful and gigantic creature has limited its present abilities by the limitations of its past. It's all because of mindset. ” [7]

WRONG THOUGHTS //

"I will never be good enough."
"I've got too many weaknesses."
"Have you seen all my secrets?"
"I come from a dysfunctional family."
"I have some major struggles."
"I'm never going to grow."

Most people struggle with their thought process. If you can get a hold of your thoughts at this moment, it can set the course for how you see your entire future. Negative thinking is what stops someone from fulfilling God's promises for their life.

Many people live much of their lives in defeat and beaten down when that was NEVER what God intended for His children!

//LET'S READ//

2 Corinthians 10:5 (ESV) -
We destroy arguments and every lofty opinion raised against the knowledge of God, and take every thought captive to obey Christ.

Colossians 3:2 (ESV) -
Set your minds on things that are above, not on things that are on earth.

Whatever has your thoughts, has your focus; and whatever has your focus, has your destiny!

Having the right mindset is vital to your success in life!

Philippians 4:8 (ESV) -

Finally, brothers, whatever is true, whatever is honorable, whatever is just, whatever is pure, whatever is lovely, whatever is commendable, if there is any excellence, if there is anything worthy of praise, think about these things.

When your mindset is on your problems more than on the promises God has for you, it's easy to lose focus on who He is and who you are because of Him. You can't have a mindset of defeat and lack and expect victory and abundance. You will produce what you are thinking about. Your thoughts have enormous power.

That's why it is important to be intentional about -

» The music you listen to.
» The movies you watch.
» The books you read.
» The shows you watch.
» The places you go.

What you think on plays a big part of who you are. With so much at stake, it's important that you guard what comes into your mind, Why? Because everything you see, hear, and feel feeds your thoughts. What you put into your mind, determines what you get out.

REMEMBER>>

The computer term **GI, GO**:

Garbage IN = Garbage OUT

You are not here to be average, you are here to be awesome! Watch your thoughts!

"Thinking is the hardest work in the world, which is probably why so few people engage in it." - Henry Ford

THINK ON IT

1. How are you going to change your mindset?

2. In order to have the right mindset, what things should you think on?

3. What daily habits can you develop to have a healthy mindset?

Notes

6

THANKFULNESS

DAY 6

THANKFULNESS

//BIG THOUGHT//

"Gratitude is the healthiest of all human emotions. The more you express gratitude for what you have, the more likely you will have even more to express gratitude for." - Zig Ziglar [8]

Every day, you take approximately 23,000 breaths, but can you remember the last time that you thanked God for those breaths? How often are you thankful? How often do you complain? Sometimes people complain so much that they don't even realize they are doing it. Now, think about this. The majority of people are not walking around pointing out everything they are thankful for. Instead, they are complaining about things that they don't have or what is missing in their life. That is because for some reason, it just seems easier or more natural to complain than to be thankful.

The truth is people are much happier when they are living a thankful life. I find that it is easier to live on the positive side of life when you are thankful. I'm not saying that life is not hard at times, but when you have a spirit of thankfulness, you can get through anything. Think about your life today. You have breath in your lungs; you are alive! You have blood in your veins. You woke up today! Even that one thing is reason enough to be thankful!

We have so much to be thankful for. The fact is that if you have asked Jesus into your heart, to be Lord and Savior of your life, then you have received the greatest gift of all time - Jesus Christ. When you invite Jesus in your life, your life is now changed. You are made new, and that means the old way of thinking and doing life is gone. **(1 Corinthians 5:17)**

(If you have never asked Jesus to be Lord and Savior and are ready to now, please flip to the back of this book for the prayer of salvation!)

Colossians 2:6-7 (ESV) -

Therefore, as you received Christ Jesus the Lord, so walk in him, rooted and built up in him and established in the faith, just as you were taught, abounding in thanksgiving.

This verse is instructing us on how we should live. It says we should live our lives in Him, rooted and built up in Him, strengthened in faith, and overflowing with thankfulness. When you are thankful, you won't be negative. In fact, you can't be. Thankful people don't complain. Isn't that a cool thing to think about? It is easy to take people for granted. It is easy at times to become angry. There are moments in life where you have negative thoughts. You must be able to control all areas of life. When you wake up in the morning, start thinking about all the great things that Christ has done for you. Start thinking and thanking Him for everything you have. This will keep your life from going negative to staying in the thankfulness of life.

Take a moment to think about all the things that you are thankful for. One time I did an exercise. I grabbed a pad of paper and a pen, and I wanted to see how many things I could write down in 5 minutes that I was thankful for. At the end of 5 minutes, I had written down over 130 things that I was thankful for. Doing an exercise like that will always help you to keep your attitude toward life in the right perspective. Thankfulness changes your perspective for the better!

Ephesians 5:20 (ESV) -

Giving thanks always and for everything to God the Father in the name of our Lord Jesus Christ.

This verse is such a great reminder to always give thanks to God. God wants His children to be thankful. Whatever you are feeling the most, or thinking about the most is what will flow out of you.

The Story of the 10 Lepers (Luke 17:12-19)

> *"Ten men came before Jesus with the hope of healing. All of them walked away cleansed, but only one turned back to praise God and thank Jesus for his Healing. Jesus makes it a point to call out the other nine who did not return, so that the importance of gratitude is shown. God deserves our thankfulness."*

ACTION STEP:
Take a moment right now to tell God the things you are thankful for. There is always something to be thankful for.

Psalm 107:1 (ESV) -

Oh give thanks to the Lord, for He is good, for His steadfast love endures forever!

There is power with a thankful heart. Give thanks with all your heart. Thankfulness is an attitude that comes out of the heart of giving thanks.

Psalms 100:1-5 (ESV) -

Make a joyful noise to the Lord, all the earth! Serve the Lord with gladness! Come into His presence with singing! Know that the Lord, He is God! It is He who made us, and we are His; we are His people, and the sheep of His pasture. Enter His gates with thanksgiving, and His courts with praise! Give thanks to Him; bless His name! For the Lord is good; His steadfast love endures forever, and His faithfulness to all generations.

Enter His gates with Thanksgiving. Start each day giving thanks.

Thankfulness turns what we don't have into enough.

THINK ON IT

Why Thankfulness?

1. Thanksgiving improves our outlook about ourselves.

2. Thanksgiving improves our outlook about our things.

3. Thanksgiving improves our outlook about our God.

Notes

7

FAITH

DAY 7

FAITH

//BIG THOUGHT//

Faith does not make things easy; it makes them possible.

> **Faith:** *belief and trust in and loyalty to God. Firm belief in something for which there is no proof. Something that is believed especially with strong conviction.*[9]

STORY//The Majestic Gazelle

"The gazelle can run up to 60 miles per hour, and while running they can turn faster than a cheetah. They roam the vast grassy plains and deserts of Africa and Asia. Their only defense against a predator is to flee. They are master escape artists! They can leap up to 15 feet high and jump over 30 feet in a single bound. Yet, these amazing animals can be raised in captivity and never know the potential that's within them. Think of gazelles you may have seen at a zoo. There is nothing but a small ditch and fence often separating you from them. You rarely ever see them run, and if you do, it's nowhere near 60 miles per hour. You don't see them jump or leap, you barely will see them stretch to eat leaves from the trees in their enclosure. If you were to visit the deserts and plains of Africa, you would see and experience a completely different animal. You would see a gazelle in the fullness of which it was designed and created to be. Wild and free. Nothing holding it back from taking the giant leaps it is designed and destined for. Don't let anything hold you back from having the faith to accomplish all that God has destined for you."

Hebrews 11:1 (ESV) -

Now faith is the assurance of things hoped for, the conviction of things not seen.

Faith is believing, trusting, and having complete confidence in someone. Who better to give your complete belief and trust to then the King of Kings and the Lord of Lords - the Almighty God! The Bible says, "And without faith it is impossible to please him…" **(Hebrews 11:6)** Our faith pleases God. When you have faith in God, and you trust Him through every trial and every circumstance, you please your Father. What you believe about God reveals how you will respond to Him. Faith plays a major role in your life.

> *"Faith takes God without any if's."* - D.L.Moody [10]

Amazing things happen when you step out in faith. Take a look at what happened to Peter when he stepped out in faith.

//LET'S READ//

Matthew 14:22-33 (ESV) -
Immediately He made the disciples get into the boat and go before Him to the other side, while He dismissed the crowds. And after He had dismissed the crowds, He went up on the mountain by Himself to pray. When evening came, He was there alone, but the boat by this time was a long way from the land, beaten by the waves, for the wind was against them. And in the fourth watch of the night He came to them, walking on the sea. But when the disciples saw Him walking on the sea, they were terrified, and said, "It is a ghost!" and they cried out in fear. But immediately Jesus spoke to them, saying, "Take heart; it is I. Do not be afraid." And Peter answered Him, "Lord, if it is you, command me to come to you on the water." He said, "Come." So, Peter got out of the boat and walked on the water and came to Jesus. But when he saw the wind, he was

afraid, and beginning to sink he cried out, "Lord, save me." Jesus immediately reached out His hand and took hold of him, saying to him, "O you of little faith, why did you doubt?" And when they got into the boat, the wind ceased. And those in the boat worshiped Him, saying, "Truly you are the Son of God."

Peter had faith in Jesus whom he kept his eyes and faith on. He didn't sink! As soon as he began to look at the storm around him and take his eyes off of Jesus, he began to sink. Peter had faith to get out of the boat, when he did, he walked on the water. Keep your eyes on Jesus and have faith!

Faith is choosing to believe what God says, in spite of what you see or feel around you.

Faith is...

Forsaking
All
I
Take
Him

Romans 1:17 (ESV) -

For in it the righteousness of God is revealed from faith for faith, as it is written, "The righteous shall live by faith."

Our day to day lives should always be a walk of faith. In order to grow from faith to faith, your faith must be exercised on a regular basis. Everyday you have an opportunity to grow in your faith. A few ways to grow your faith is through praying, reading God's Word, being a part of a church community, listening to worship music, spending time with the right people, focusing on the positive and dreaming big. Trust in the Lord and be determined to walk in faith all of your days and watch what God will do. 2 Corinthians 5:7 says, "for we walk by faith, not by sight." That is how to live your life by faith!

THINK ON IT

"Faith places no limitations on God, and God places no limitations on faith."
- Jenetzen Franklin [11]

1. What are things you can do daily to grow your faith?

2. Through faith we need to believe big.

3. What are some things you are believing in faith for?

Notes

8

GOD FIRST

DAY 8

GOD FIRST

//BIG THOUGHT//

You will never ever be in second place by choosing to put God first every day.

Matthew 6:33 (ESV) -

But seek first the kingdom of God and His righteousness, and all these things will be added to you.

Putting God first is so important in your life. It is the foundation of growing your relationship with Him. Do you know that God desires to be first in your life? He longs to spend time with you every day. You are His child, and He loves you so much. You are His Son or Daughter. Just like He knows you, He wants you to know Him personally.

Your life foundation needs to be built on Him.

STORY // Matthew 7:24-27 (ESV) -

"Everyone then who hears these words of mine and does them will be like a wise man who built his house on the rock. And the rain fell, and the floods came, and the winds blew and beat on that house, but it did not fall, because it had been founded on the rock. And everyone who hears these words of mine and does not do them will be like a foolish man who built his house on the sand. And the rain fell, and the floods came, and the winds blew and beat against that house, and it fell, and great was the fall of it."

When you put God first you are building your house (your life) on the Rock, the Rock of Christ. The Bible says in Ephesians 2:20, that Christ Jesus is the cornerstone that we are to build our foundation on. Jesus is our Cornerstone, our essential piece, our core; He is our strong foundation! As you spend time with Him and grow in your relationship with Him, your foundation grows deeper and gets stronger. There are times in life that you can put other things before God like...

Yourself
Friends
Jobs
Sports
Social Media

God wants to be the center of your life. He wants to be at the core of who you are. I want to challenge you to put Him first, to make Him the priority and focus every day in your life. When you put God first, all other things fall into place.

//LET'S READ//

Matthew 6:24 (ESV) -

No one can serve two masters, for either he will hate the one and love the other, or he will be devoted to the one and despise the other. You cannot serve God and money.

Matthew 6:21(ESV) -

For where your treasure is, there your heart will be also.

STORY // The Leaning Tower of Pisa

"Scientists travel every year to the city of Pisa in Northern Italy to measure the buildings slow descent. They report that the 179-foot tower built in 1173, moves about one-twentieth of an inch per year. It is now 17 feet out of plumb (alignment). Recent renovations may have saved the 810 year old tower and prevented it from collapsing. Pisa means marshy land. Did you know that the tower began to lean before the builders completed building it? In fact, the foundation is only 10 feet deep! The Leaning Tower of Pisa leans, because it is built on faulty foundation. In life, if God isn't your number one priority, your foundation will be faulty and unsteady. Your foundation needs to be built on the Word of God. When your foundation is built on God, it will be strong and able to withstand anything that may be thrown at it."[12]

THINK ON IT –

Put God first and build your foundation on the one and only true Rock!

Notes

9

FEAR NOT

DAY 9

FEAR NOT

//BIG THOUGHT//
The fears we don't face become our limits.

> **Fear has two meanings:** *Forget Everything And Run or Face Everything And Rise*

The choice is yours!

What are you afraid of?

There was an article published about the top 5 fears shared by people everywhere. [13]

1. Spiders
2. Snakes
3. Heights
4. Open or Crowded Spaces
5. Dogs

e all at some level have dealt with fears in our lives, but it is important to know that God does NOT give you fear.

2 Timothy 1:7 (NLT) -
For God gave us a spirit not of fear but of power and love and self-control.

We do not have to fear when we know that we have God on our side.

STORY //

"Back in 2006, there was a little three year old girl who was playing on her family's farm. She wandered into the cornfield and before she knew it, she was lost. People from all over the area came to help search

for the lost little girl. They spent over 12 hours searching through the large cornfields. After a while, they were able to locate her. She was terrified and afraid, yet so happy to see people. The amazing thing about this story is that people came together to find this little girl. Do you know what else is amazing? When you have fear that tries to grip your heart or terrifies you, God is always with you. He never leaves your side. You have nothing to fear. ❞ [14]

When I was a kid, we sang this song in the church I went to. The chorus was "Fear not for I am with you, fear not for I am with you, fear not for I am with you says the Lord". This has stuck with me for over twenty years. Probably because we sang it every single Sunday for just about ten years. There is so much truth and power in this chorus. The Bible talks about not being afraid but trusting in the Lord.

John 14:1 (ESV) -

Let not your hearts be troubled. Believe in God; believe also in me.

The enemy wants to grip your heart with fear and doubt, but Jesus says to believe in Him and not be troubled. Trust that He will be there with you. Trust that He is your help and your guide.

David often leads us in a prayer to not fear. Many times in the book of Psalms, you see David crying out to the Lord in prayer, and many times you find him expressing his trust in the Lord.

One example is Psalm 56. David has been seized by the Philistines, and he starts to become afraid, but instead of giving into his fear, he sets his eyes on the Lord. He praises God, and God's word to him is: FEAR NOT! David chose to put his trust in the Lord.

Psalm 56:3-4 (ESV) -

When I am afraid, I put my trust in you. In God, whose word I praise, in God I trust; I shall not be afraid. What can flesh do to me?

Take a Deeper Look //

Isaiah 41:10 (ESV)
1 John 4:18 (ESV)
Hebrews 13:6 (ESV)
Matthew 14:22-36 (ESV)

Have courage, because Jesus is with you. The fears we choose not to face, become our limits in life. Never let your fear decide your fate. Don't let fear imprison you. God has given you freedom over fear. FEAR NOT!

STORY // From Fear to Faith - Luke 8:49-56 (ESV)

> *"While He was still speaking, someone from the ruler's house came and said, "Your daughter is dead; do not trouble the Teacher any more." But Jesus on hearing this answered Him, "Do not fear; only believe, and she will be well." And when He came to the house, He allowed no one to enter with Him, except Peter and John and James, and the father and mother of the child. And all were weeping and mourning for her, but He said, "Do not weep, for she is not dead but sleeping." And they laughed at Him, knowing that she was dead. But taking her by the hand He called, saying, "Child, arise." And her spirit returned, and she got up at once. And He directed that something should be given her to eat. And her parents were amazed, but He charged them to tell no one what had happened."*

When fear tries to grip your heart, repeat the following confession and believe what you say!

//CONFESSION//

I will trust the Lord.
I will not let fear grip my heart.
I will not let fear have control over my life.
I will not live in fear.
The Lord is my strength.
He is my help.
He is my Rock.
He is my foundation.
I will trust in Him!

There's always going to be fearful situations, but remember the words of Jesus. Do not fear-just trust Me. His desire is that you move from fear to faith. Jesus is the only one who can calm your fears, because He alone conquered the grave. As the earlier verse says, "Let not your hearts be troubled. Believe in God; believe also in me." **John 14:1 (ESV)**

THINK ON IT

What are you afraid of? What fear is trying to take ahold of you right now? What hardship or trouble are you facing?

Nothing is bigger than the God who made the heavens and the earth, so there is nothing to fear. He is on YOUR side.

Pray with David. "When I am afraid of ______, I will trust in you, O Lord."

Notes

10

WORDS

DAY 10

WORDS

//BIG THOUGHT//

Words are like an elevator; they can bring you up, or bring you down. Words have power!

THE OLD SAYING:
Sticks and stones may break my bones, but words will never hurt me.

That is a BIG FAT LIE! Words have power! They can heal, or they can hurt. Words have started wars. Words are more powerful than any weapon on planet earth. There are people today who are getting professional help, because of the words that have been spoken over them. Make sure you choose your words wisely, and be sure to taste your words before you spit them out. Words have the power to bring health or hurt, life or death.

Healthy Words	Hurtful Words
You're Awesome	You're Ugly
You're Powerful	You're Stupid
You're Beautiful	You're Crazy
You're Wonderful	You're Gross
You're Fantastic	You're Weak
You're Amazing	You're Disgusting
You're Incredible	You're Trash
You're Strong	You're Broken
You're Smart	You're Unwanted
You're Lovely	You're Worthless

Proverbs 18:21 (ESV) -

Death and life are in the power of the tongue, and those who love it will eat its fruits.

Proverbs 6:2 (ESV) -

If you are snared in the words of your mouth, caught in the words of your mouth.

STORY //

"There was a father who traveled all the time, and when he would come off the road, he would take his small son to his favorite restaurant where he would get his little meal. On this particular time, the father felt compelled to encourage his son. As he began to encourage, the son's countenance began to change. He began to tell his son how awesome, incredible, and fantastic he was. The little boy had such a huge grin on his face. The father went to take a bite of his food, and the little son's hand reached up and knocked the food out of his dad's hand. The son said, "Tell me more! Tell me more!" There is so much power in the way we use our words. The father was emotionally nourishing his son by the words he was using." [15]

Proverbs 12:18 (ESV) -

There is one whose rash words are like sword thrusts, but the tongue of the wise brings healing.

God desires for us to always speak life and always bring healing. Speak positivity, not negativity. Speak hope and not fear. Speak life and not death.

Harvard business review did a study on the power of positive words in ratio to the negative. They found that it takes just about 6 positive phrases or words of affirmation to produce success and productivity. We must be positive speakers if we are to see positivity in our lives. [13]

James 3:5-6 (ESV) -

So also the tongue is a small member, yet it boasts of great things. How great a forest is set ablaze by such a small fire! And the tongue is a fire, a world of unrighteousness. The tongue is set among our members, staining the whole body, setting on fire the entire course of life, and set on fire by hell.

The tongue is a small thing, but what enormous damage it can do. However, the tongue also has the power to bring life and to repair the damage done. Remember, once you let words out of your mouth, you can never put them back in again. Look for ways to encourage others with your words. Be a life-giver.

STORY //

> *"On Sunday evening, October 8, 1871, the Chicago fire started in the barn of Patrick and Catherine O'Leary. The story goes that Mrs. O'Leary lit a lantern in her barn and one of her cows kicked it over. It took two days for the fire to be put out. By the time they put out the fire, it had damaged 3 and 1/3 square miles and destroyed over $192,000,000 in property. 100,000 people were left homeless, and 300 people lost their lives. All because of one small spark; one small lantern."* [16]

Matthew 12:37 (ESV) -

For by your words you will be justified, and by your words you will be condemned.

We need to work on making sure that our speech and self-talk is uplifting and brings good fruit.

We need to build a firewall in our speech!

> *"A word once uttered can never be recalled."*
> - Horace, Italian Poet [17]

Colossians 4:5-6 (ESV) -

Walk in wisdom toward outsiders, making the best use of the time. Let your speech always be gracious, seasoned with salt, so that you may know how you ought to answer each person.

THINK ON IT -

1. How can you use the words you speak to bring life and not death to those around you?

Notes

Notes

11

ATTITUDE

DAY 11

ATTITUDE

//BIG THOUGHT//

The only difference between a good day and a bad day is your Attitude.

STORY //

> *"There were once two lost frogs who couldn't find their way back to their pond. They hopped here, and they hopped there, but they were decidedly lost. They were lost and beginning to get very thirsty. They saw a large pot of cream, and jumped into it. As soon as they hit the sticky liquid, they knew they made a mistake. This was not a pond at all, but a bucket of cream! It was thick cream that was beginning to pull them under! They tried to scramble up the side of the pot, but the cream made them slip down.*
>
> *After some time one of the frogs said, "It is no use; we are going to die." The other frog said, "Don't give up, change your attitude!" After a while, the one frog gave up and was no longer seen, but the other frog kept swimming, and after quite a while the cream became harder and harder until it turned into butter, and he was able to hop out and continue on his way."* [18]

His Attitude was the determining factor between life and death! It is a positive attitude towards life that can change your outlook or perspective on a situation.

Your Attitude is important, your Attitude can...

Make you or Break you
Heal you or Hurt you
Make you Successful or a Failure
Give you Friends or Enemies
Make you Happy or Miserable.

Ephesians 5:1 (ESV) -

Therefore, be imitators of God, as beloved children.

It is up to you to have the right attitude in life and to do your best to be like Christ. Take a look at this story and see what the wrong outlook or attitude can look like.

Attitude is everything.

STORY //

"Once a cranky grandpa laid down to take a nap. To have a little fun, his grandson put some hamburger cheese (smelly cheese) on his mustache, right under his nose. Grandpa awoke with a snort, staggered out of the bedroom and shouted, "This room stinks!" All through the house he went shouting, louder, "This whole house stinks!" He charged out on the porch and shouted as loud as he could, "The whole world stinks." " [19]

The truth is, it was grandpa who stunk. The problem was right under his own nose. 95 times out of 100, when you begin to feel that the things in life stink, the problem is not with the world or with others, but with yourself. The problem is that your attitude has become negative. Change your negative attitude to a positive one, and you can change your world. Attitude is always our choice. Attitude is everything.

"Your attitude, not your aptitude, will determine your altitude."
- Zig Ziglar [20]

"Attitude is a little thing that makes a big difference."
- Winston Churchill [21]

Matthew 20:29-34 (ESV) -

And as they went out of Jericho, a great crowd followed him. And behold, there were two blind men sitting by the roadside, and when they heard that Jesus was passing by, they cried out, "Lord, have mercy on us, Son of David!" The crowd rebuked them, telling them to be silent, but they cried out all the more, "Lord, have mercy on us, Son of David!" And stopping, Jesus called them and said, "What do you want me to do for you?" They said to him, "Lord, let our eyes be opened." And Jesus in pity touched their eyes, and immediately they recovered their sight and followed him.

A positive attitude leads to positive outcomes. As you read in the story, the blind men kept a positive attitude not only towards their situation but the power of Christ. They chose to not let the power of others and their attitudes effect the outcome of their blindness. They chose to stay positive and to pursue Christ. There is only one good thing about a bad attitude, and that is you have the power to change it to a positive attitude. The outcome of your situation is determined by the attitude you choose to take towards your situation and the power of God.

TAKE A DEEPER LOOK //

> Proverbs 17:22 (ESV)
> Philippians 2:14 (ESV)
> Philippians 4:8-9 (ESV)
> Philippians 2:5 (ESV)

THINK ON IT -

3 Points about Your Attitude:

1. Your Attitude reveals what is going on inside you.
2. Your Attitude will affect every relationship in your life.
3. Your Attitude is always your choice.

Notes

Notes

12

CHOICES

DAY 12

CHOICES

//BIG THOUGHT//

"Life is a matter of choices, and every choice you make makes you."

- John C Maxwell [22]

Life is about making choices. Every day we have a choice to make, and every choice is important. The choices we make determine our destiny. Think about the choices you make everyday -

» To get up or sleep in
» To go to school or stay home
» To go to work or not go to work
» The right friends or the wrong friends
» Positive thoughts or negative thoughts
» Good attitude or bad attitude.

Deuteronomy 30:15 (ESV) -

See, I have set before you today life and good, death and evil. If you obey the commandments of the Lord your God that I command you today, by loving the Lord your God, by walking in His ways, and by keeping His commandments and His statutes and His rules, then you shall live and multiply, and the Lord your God will bless you in the land that you are entering to take possession of it.

Every day is all about making choices. It is important that we strive to make choices that are pleasing to the Lord. The most important choice you can make is to put Jesus first every day. In the game of life, you are not born a winner, you are not born a loser, but you are born a chooser. You have the power of choice on the inside of you. The choices you make will make you - good or bad, right or wrong.

STORY // The Choices of the Lost Son
(Luke 15:11-27 NLT)

"*And he said, "There was a man who had two sons. And the younger of them said to his father, 'Father, give me the share of property that is coming to me.' And he divided his property between them. Not many days later, the younger son gathered all he had and took a journey into a far country, and there he squandered his property in reckless living. And when he had spent everything, a severe famine arose in that country, and he began to be in need. So he went and hired himself out to one of the citizens of that country, who sent him into his fields to feed pigs. And he was longing to be fed with the pods that the pigs ate, and no one gave him anything. But when he came to himself, he said, 'How many of my father's hired servants have more than enough bread, but I perish here with hunger! I will arise and go to my father, and I will say to him, "Father, I have sinned against heaven and before you. I am no longer worthy to be called your son. Treat me as one of your hired servants."' And he arose and came to his father. But while he was still a long way off, his father saw him and felt compassion, and ran and embraced him and kissed him. And the son said to him, 'Father, I have sinned against heaven and before you. I am no longer worthy to be called your son.' But the father said to his servants, 'Bring quickly the best robe, and put it on him, and put a ring on his hand, and shoes on his feet. And bring the fattened calf and kill it, and let us eat and celebrate. For this my son was dead, and is alive again; he was lost, and is found.' And they began to celebrate. Now his older son was in the field, and as he came and drew near to the house, he heard music and dancing. And he called one of the servants and asked what these things meant. And he said to him, 'Your brother has come, and your father has killed the fattened calf, because he has received him back safe and sound.'*"

The son's decisions formed who he became - lost, alone, starving, and desperate. The choices you make in life will ultimately form your future. What choices are you making today to prepare you for the future you see for yourself?

Columbia University researcher Sheena Iyengar has found that the average person makes about 70 decisions every day. That's 25,500 decisions a year.

Over 70 years, that is 1,788,500 decisions.

Albert Camus said "Life is a sum of all your choices." [23]

You put all of those 1,788,500 choices together, and that's who you are.

Galatians 6:7-8 (ESV) -

Do not be deceived: God is not mocked, for whatever one sows, that will he also reap. For the one who sows to his own flesh will from the flesh reap corruption, but the one who sows to the Spirit will from the Spirit reap eternal life.

Your choices have consequences. Bad or good, you will reap what you sow. Meaning if you sow bad, you will reap bad. If you sow good, you will reap good. It is always about choices.

STORY //

> *"A farmer hired a man to work for him. He told him his first task would be to paint the barn and said it should take him about three days to complete. But the hired man was finished in one day. The farmer set him to cutting wood, telling him it would require about 4 days. The hired man finished in a day and a half, to the farmer's amazement. The next task was to sort out a large pile of potatoes. He was to arrange them into three piles: seed potatoes, food for the hogs, and potatoes that were good enough to sell. The farmer said it was a small job and shouldn't take long at all. At the end of the day the farmer came back and found the hired man had barely started. 'What's the matter here' the farmer asked. 'I can work hard, but I can't make decisions!'"* [24]

Making the right decision (choice) is one of the biggest pieces of success.

"Your attitude can take you forward or your attitude can take you down. The choice is always yours!"
- Catherine Pulsifer [25]

"In every single thing, you do, you are choosing a direction. Your life is a product of choices."
- Dr. Kathleen Hall [25]

Change begins with a choice!

Every morning in Africa, a gazelle wakes up. It knows it must run faster than the fastest lion or it will be killed. Every morning a lion wakes up; it knows it must outrun the slowest gazelle, or it will starve to death. It doesn't matter whether you are a lion or a gazelle - when the sun comes up – YOU HAVE A CHOICE! [25]

THINK ON IT

What choices are you making everyday to become better?

____

____

____

____

____

____

____

____

____

____

____

Notes

13

PERSEVERENCE

DAY 13

PERSEVERENCE

//BIG THOUGHT//

Perseverance is the hard work you do after you get tired of doing the hard work you already did. -Newt Gingrich [28]

Perseverance: *Doing something despite difficulties or delays in achieving success.* [29]

It is important in life to always find a way to win, trust the process, work hard, be committed to finish the task, the dream, the job, the career. It is important to know that you can win in life. That no matter what you are facing, you have the ability to win. You are more than a conqueror! (Romans 8:37, ESV)

STORY // Jesus Calms the Storm - (Matthew 8:23-27 ESV)

> "*And when He got into the boat, His disciples followed Him. And behold, there arose a great storm on the sea, so that the boat was being swamped by the waves; but he was asleep. And they went and woke him, saying, "Save us, Lord; we are perishing." And he said to them, "Why are you afraid, O you of little faith?" Then he rose and rebuked the winds and the sea, and there was a great calm. And the men marveled, saying, "What sort of man is this, that even winds and sea obey him?"*"

There are times in life that we go through certain storms. The only way to come out of the storm and be victorious, is through perseverance. Tough times don't last, tough people do. Don't tell God how great your storm is, tell your storm how great God is. Tell the storm to be still.

Galatians 6:9 (ESV) -

And let us not grow weary of doing good, for in due season we will reap, if we do not give up.

STORY // Henry Ford

> *"Automobile genius Henry Ford once came up with a revolutionary plan for a new kind of engine which we know today as the V-8. Ford was eager to get his great new idea into production. He had some men draw up the plans, and present them to the engineers. As the engineers studied the drawings, one by one they came to the same conclusion. Their visionary boss just didn't know much about the fundamental principles of engineering. He'd have to be told gently, that his dream was impossible. Ford said, "Produce it anyway." They replied, "But it's impossible." "Go ahead," Ford commanded, "and stay on the job until you succeed, no matter how much time is required."*
>
> *For six months they struggled with drawing after drawing, design after design. Nothing. Another six months. Nothing. At the end of the year Ford checked with his engineers and they once again told him that what he wanted was impossible. Ford told them to keep going. They did, and soon they discovered how to build a V-8 engine."*
>
> - Napolean Hill, Think and Grow Rich, 1960 [30]

Romans 5:4 (ESV) -

and endurance produces character, and character produces hope.

Perseverance – if life knocks you down, do you stay down or get back up? How many times do you keep getting back up? Perseverance causes you to keep moving, keep getting back up, and moving past things that are thrown at you.

Micah 7:8 (ESV) -

Rejoice not over me, O my enemy; when I fall, I shall rise; when I sit in darkness, the Lord will be a light to me.

> *"By perseverance the snail reached the ark."*
> – Charles Spurgeon [31]

STORY //

> *"One time there was a man who was lost in a snowstorm. He could only see a few feet in front of him. This man walked for hours in the blizzardy snowstorm. Finally, he stumbled and fell into the snow. He thought, "I'm too tired! I can't lift myself up. I'll just sleep for a few moments. Maybe then I can get going again." But suddenly, he realized that the object over which he had stumbled was a body. He began to brush away the snow and found that the body still had a pulse - He was still alive. "Oh, I've got to help him. I've got to save him!"*
>
> *In a super-human effort, the man stood to his feet, put the body over his shoulders, and started walking through the blizzard once more. In just a few more yards, he came to a cabin where he found safety from the storm. The man found that he was saved by saving another.*
>
> *The man persevered his way through the snowstorm. At first, he was going to let the snowstorm stop him from moving, but he pushed through and at the end of it, he found what he was looking for."*

James 1:12 (ESV) -

Blessed is the man who remains steadfast under trial, for when he has stood the test he will receive the crown of life, which God has promised to those who love him.

THINK ON IT -

Do you recall a time in your life where you had to have perseverance?

____

____

____

Notes

Notes

14

I AM'S

DAY 14

I AM'S

//BIG THOUGHT//

People's opinion of me doesn't define who I AM; who I AM comes from who HE is!

The God of the universe calls Himself - "I AM".

Exodus 3:13-14 (ESV) -

God said to Moses, "I am who I am." And he said, "Say this to the people of Israel: 'I am has sent me to you.'" God also said to Moses, "Say this to the people of Israel: 'The Lord, the God of your fathers, the God of Abraham, the God of Isaac, and the God of Jacob, has sent me to you.' This is my name forever, and thus I am to be remembered throughout all generations.

Seven times in the Gospel of John, Jesus said "I AM". He said…

I AM the bread of life. **(John 6:35)**
- » Jesus is your sustainer.

I AM the light of the world. **(John 8:12)**
- » Jesus is your source of truth.

I AM the door. **(John 10:9)**
- » Jesus is the only door you can go through to find true salvation.

I AM the true vine. **(John 15:1)**
- » Jesus is the one who nourishes and sustains your soul.

I AM the good shepherd. **(John 10:11)**
- » - Jesus is the one who takes care of your every need.

I AM the resurrection and the life. **(John 11:25)**
- » - Jesus is the one who brings life in the midst of death.

I AM the way, the truth, and the life. **(John 14:6)**
- » - Jesus is the source of everything.

No one can ever be fully satisfied with anything less than Jesus Christ!

It is so important to know who you are. When you know who you are, you will know where you are going in life. Jesus knows who He is, and you need to know who you are with Him.

So, who are you? What are your I AM's?

Take a look at who God says you are //

- » You are a child of God. **(Romans 8:16)**
- » You are redeemed from the hand of the enemy. **(Psalms 107:2)**
- » You are a new creature. **(2 Corinthians 5:17)**
- » You are an imitator of Jesus. **(Ephesians 5:1)**
- » You are justified. **(Romans 5:1)**
- » You are more than a conqueror. **(Romans 8:37)**
- » You are the light of the world. **(Matthew 5:14)**
- » You are not moved by what you see. **(2 Corinthians 4:18)**
- » You are above only and not beneath. **(Deuteronomy 28:13)**
- » You are an heir of eternal life. **(1 John 5:11-12)**

STORY //

> *"During a motivational lecture at a school, a girl stood up and yelled, "I know who I am!" Some of the girls around her, began to laugh. She was very young and filled with passion. Her dream was to be a professional singer. She stood there knowing who she was even though her peers were laughing at her. The speaker stopped his lecture and said, "Knowing who you are is the most important thing in life." It has been said that this girl went on to fulfill her dream of becoming a singer."*

//CONFESSION//

- I AM kingdom minded.
- I AM a servant leader.
- I AM a leader of leaders.
- I AM a world-changer.
- I AM a life-time learner.
- I AM an energy producer.
- I AM a motivator.
- I AM a difference maker.
- I AM an odds defier.
- I AM a winner.
- I AM faithful.
- I AM strong.
- I AM dependable.
- I AM honest.
- I AM alert.
- I AM unstoppable.
- I AM creative.
- I AM passionate.
- I AM honorable.

THINK ON IT

Just like Jesus had his 7 I Am's, what are your I Am's?

15

LEADERSHIP

DAY 15

LEADERSHIP

//BIG THOUGHT//

"A leader is one who knows the way, goes the way, and shows the way."

- John C. Maxwell [32]

STORY //

"*Every year geese fly their way to a warmer climate. They often cover thousands of miles before reaching their destination. Have you ever studied why they fly as they do? It is fascinating to read what has been discovered about their flight pattern and their in-flight habits. Four come to mind.*

Those in front rotate their leadership. When one lead goose gets tired, it changes places with one in the wing of the V-formation and another will fly point.

By flying as they do, the members of the flock create an upward air current for one another. Each flap of the wings literally creates an uplift for the bird immediately following.

When one goose gets sick or wounded, two fall out of formation with it and follow it down to help and protect it. They stay with the struggler until it's able to fly again.

The geese in the rear of the formation are the ones who do the honking. The repeated honks encourage those in front to stay at it. One lesson stands out above all others: it is the natural instinct of geese to work together. Whether it's rotating, flapping, helping, or simply honking, the flock is in it together... which enables them to accomplish what they set out to do." [33]

Great leaders lead the way. A great leader is one who is able to motivate people; one who is capable of making good decisions, even under pressure or in conditions of uncertainty; one who can guide people through action as well as encourages. The heart of a leader is the foundation; it is what drives their passion for the Lord. The leader is always the one who encourages.

Matthew 6:33 (ESV) -

But seek first the kingdom of God and his righteousness, and all these things will be added to you.

1. Yes, you are called to be a leader.

In many ways, the call to follow and put Jesus first is a call to leadership.

Remember, that Jesus didn't just save you from something. He saved you for something. Being a leader isn't just about standing on a stage and talking to a room filled with people. Being a leader is following Jesus every day. The disciples weren't the most gifted leaders, yet God used these men to change the world. Following Jesus is not for some elite or few, following Jesus is for everyone. Jesus turned ordinary men into world-changers. If Jesus could use them, you can't say He can't use you. You are a leader, and you have to see yourself that way. Everyday you have to lead yourself to be the leader God has called you to be.

Leaders believe there is a way.
Leaders always believe there is an answer.
Leaders always are encouraging.
Leaders role with a spirit of excellence.
Leaders have a positive attitude.
Leaders maintain a healthy lifestyle.
Leaders have the right people in their life.
Leaders live by the Word of God.
Leaders spend time with Jesus.
Leaders find a way to win.

2. Great leaders go after God with all their heart.

Hebrews 13:7 (ESV) -

Remember your leaders, those who spoke to you the word of God. Consider the outcome of their way of life, and imitate their faith.

John 3:30 (ESV) -

He must increase, but I must decrease.

A great leader understands that Jesus has to be number one in his life in order to become all that Jesus has called him to be. Great leaders lead themselves every day to put God first, to passionately seek the Lord all the time. Go after God with everything you have. The Bible says in Proverbs 3:5-6, "*Trust in the Lord with all your heart, and do not lean on your own understanding. In all your ways acknowledge him, and he will make straight your paths.*"

STORY //

"*During the 19th century, Ireland was stricken by a potato famine. During this time, many of the Irish people immigrated to America. A young Irish boy stowed away on an America-bound ship. At sea, the ship struck an iceberg and began to sink. As people scrambled frantically for the lifeboats, the captain supervised the activity and was the last to leave the sinking vessel. When he looked back at the ship, he saw the young stowaway coming out of hiding.*

The brave captain ordered his lifeboat back to the sinking ship. He climbed aboard and rescued the boy, putting him in the seat the captain had vacated - the only available place in the lifeboat. As the lifeboat slowly pulled away from the sinking ship, the captain yelled out to the boy, "Son, never forget what has been done for you today!"" [34]

Always remember that others have paved the way before you, so that you can lead as God has called you to lead. Every leadership platform that you have, someone has gone before you to pave the way. Never forget those who have gone before you, and the price that was paid to allow you the opportunity.

THINK ON IT

1. How can you grow your leadership?

2. What are ways you can help others grow in their leadership?

Notes

Notes

16

LIFE

DAY 16

LIFE

//BIG THOUGHT//

"The mission in life is not merely to survive, but to thrive; and to do so with some passion, some compassion, some humor and some style. "

– Maya Angelou [35]

Life is so precious; it is a gift from God. You should always honor life and never take it for granted. If you don't do something with life, life will do something with you. Life needs to be valued. God has a plan and a purpose for your life. Life is so precious; it is not meant to just exist, but to live life with purpose.

James 4:14 (ESV) –

Yet you do not know what tomorrow will bring. What is your life? For you are a mist that appears for a little time and then vanishes.

Proverbs 27:1 (ESV) –

Do not boast about tomorrow, for you do not know what a day may bring.

STORY //

"Stop! In the name of Christ, stop!" People watched as a man jumped on the railing, ran onto the field, held up his hands, and shouted, "Stop! In the name of Christ, stop!" He ran in between two combatants, 2 gladiators who were fighting to the death, and he begged them to stop.

Who was this man? His name was Telemachus.

Telemachus was a monk who lived in a cloistered monastery somewhere in eastern Europe in the late 4th century. He felt God say to him, "Go to Rome." So, he put his possessions in a bag and set off for Rome. When he arrived in the city on January 1, 404, people were thronging in the streets. He asked what all the excitement was about, and was told that this was the day the gladiators would be fighting to the death in the Roman Coliseum.

He thought to himself, 4 centuries after Christ, and they are still killing each other, for enjoyment. He ran into the Coliseum, and as he arrived he heard the gladiators say, "Hail to Caesar! We are for Caesar!" He thought, "This is not right." That's when he jumped over the railing and went out into the middle of the field, got between 2 gladiators, held up his hands, and shouted, "Stop! In the name of Christ, stop!"

How did the crowd respond? The crowd protested and began to shout, "Run him through! Run him through!" A gladiator came over and hit Telemachus in the stomach with the back of his sword. It sent him sprawling in the sand. Telemachus got up and stood between the gladiators again, and shouted, "Stop! In the name of Christ, stop!" But the crowd chanted louder and louder, "Run him through! Run him through! Run him through!" One gladiator came over and thrust his sword through the little monk's stomach, and he fell into the sand, which began to turn crimson with his blood. One last time he gasped out, "Stop! In the name of Christ, stop!" A hush came over 80,000 people in the Coliseum. Then, a man stood up and left. Then another and another and within minutes all 80,000 people walked out of the coliseum. It was the last known gladiatorial contest in the Roman empire. Three days later, the Roman Emperor Honorius declared Telemachus a martyr, and officially ended all gladiatorial contests. ” [36]

Can one person make a difference with their life? Telemachus was appalled by what He saw in the Roman Coliseum. He could not believe that 4 centuries after Christ, people were still killing each other for pleasure. He chose to make his life count, and take a stand for life. God has called you to make a difference with your life. Your life is a gift from God. You are not here to just merely exist, but you are here to live. There is a reason and a purpose that you are alive. There is greatness in you.

Jeremiah 29:11 (ESV) -

For I know the plans I have for you, declares the Lord, plans for welfare and not for evil, to give you a future and a hope.

> *"I'm going to make everything around me beautiful - that will be my life."* - Elsie De Wolfe [37]

Life is a gift; wake up every day and realize that. The enemy wants to take you out of the game called life. Do NOT allow him to have that power. You have power over the enemy.

John 10:10 (ESV) -

The thief comes only to steal and kill and destroy. I came that they may have life and have it abundantly.

Jesus came to give us all a life of purpose. Life is a gift. Make it count and use your life to make a difference!

//CONFESSION//

My life is full of unlimited possibilities.
My life is blessed.
My life is beautiful.
My life is full of favor.
My life is amazing.
My life is important.
My life is awesome.
Life is a gift from God.
I do not take life for granted.

THINK ON IT

Every morning, wake up and thank God for the gift of life! Don't take life for granted, and don't get caught up in life's drama. Value and make the most of every day you have.

Notes

Notes

17

GROWTH

DAY 17

GROWTH

//BIG THOUGHT//

Growth isn't for everybody. Some people just want to stay the same forever.

Living things grow - whether they are plants, animals, or humans; growth is a normal part of existence. Jesus wants us to grow. He wants us to grow our faith, in our love walk, and in our knowledge of the Word of God. Growth is not automatic; it happens with intentionality, with a plan. A lot of people don't grow, because they don't have a plan to grow. We grow spiritually by praying, reading the Bible, reading books, being around the right people, and the list can go on. It's never too late to learn or to grow. It doesn't matter how old or how young you are, you can always grow. Unteachable is unusable. Commit in your heart to be a lifetime learner. Make a commitment every day to go to the next level. It's not going to be easy, and it will definitely be hard; but it will be well worth it.

STORY //

"I heard about a police officer who stopped a car that was filled with elderly ladies. The car was going too slow on the highway. The officer came up to the car and talked to the driver. The conversation went something like this. The officer asked, "Why are you driving so slow?" She replied, "Well officer, I've seen all these signs along the way that say 20, and that's what I've been doing. I've been going 20." The officer replied, "Those are signs indicating the number of the highway. It is highway 20." She responded, "Thank you so much. I didn't realize that." But then the officer looked in the back seat, and he noticed 3 elderly ladies with panicked looks on their faces and white knuckles from having to hold on to one another to tightly.

The officer looked back at the driver and said, "What's wrong with these ladies in the back seat?" "Oh, officer, you see, we just got off highway 101 a few miles ago."" [38]

That's a funny little story, but the point is that you always have the ability and potential to grow and to learn new things! So, choose to grow! If you will grow in God, then you will grow spiritually.

James 4:8 (ESV) -

Draw near to God, and He will draw near to you...

As you draw close to God, you will grow!

2 Peter 3:18 (ESV) -

But grow in the grace and knowledge of our Lord and Savior Jesus Christ. To Him be the glory both now and to the day of eternity. Amen.

The fact that the Bible says you must grow in the grace and knowledge of our Lord indicates a process. It doesn't just happen. It takes time. When you grow, everything around you will grow.

In high school, you take algebra and learn the formula for distance –

R x T= D
Rate x Time = Distance

This formula means that if someone is going 5 miles per hour, it will take that individual 1,000 hours to cover 5,000 miles. It means that if someone is going 50 miles per hour, it will take that person 100 hours to cover 5,000 miles. It means that if the same person is going 500 miles per hour, it will take that person 10 hours to cover 5,000 miles.

There are some people in the faith that have known the Lord for 50 years. By now they should be matured, but they are putting along at 1 mile per hour. Some may even have stalled out and are not going anywhere just sitting there, causing a traffic jam behind them. There is no shortcut to growth. There is no instant pill. Growth takes effort, time, and a plan.

Ephesians 4:15 ESV -

Rather, speaking the truth in love, we are to grow up in every way into Him who is the head, into Christ.

You must know how to grow yourself. You must have self-awareness to know where you are in life. The first step to true growth is being honest with yourself. In order for a muscle to grow, it has to be pushed, stretched, have rest, and have the proper nourishment. There are some necessary things required in order for your spirit to grow.

THINK ON IT

TRY THESE WAYS TO GROW //

» Reading God's Word
» Praying
» Worshipping the Lord
» Taking Bible Classes
» Studying Growth Resources

Notes

18

FRIENDS

DAY *18*

FRIENDS

//BIG THOUGHT//

The voices will determine your choices. Be careful who you're listening to.

The Bible tells us that we get to decide whether we'll walk with the wise or flounder with fools. (*Proverbs 13:20 - "Whoever walks with the wise becomes wise, but the companion of fools will suffer harm."*) What impact have your friends had on you lately? Friends influence you - for better or the worse - more than you think. The Bible tells us that as iron sharpens iron, and one man sharpens another **(Proverbs 27:17 ESV).**

It really does matter which friends you spend time with. Surround yourself with people that encourage you and inspire you. The friends you hang out with are a prophecy of your future.

Surround yourself with great people.

> *"A leader's potential is determined by those closest to them."*
> – John C Maxwell, The Law of the Inner Circle [39]

You rise or fall to the level of the people around you!

There's a saying, "Show me your friends and I'll show you your future." It is so very important to associate with people that inspire you, people that challenge you to rise higher, people that make you better. Don't waste your valuable time with people that don't have your best interest in mind. Your destiny is too important.

> *"You are the average of the 5 people you spend the most time with."* – Jim Rohn [40]

What is a true friend?

- » A true friend is someone who brags about your strengths and defends your weaknesses.
- » A true friend is someone who will be there on the good days and the bad days.
- » A true friend will always push you to be better.
- » A true friend will seek to make you better.
- » A true friend will always encourage you.
- » A true friend will support you.
- » A true friend will believe the best.
- » A true friend will empower you.

STORY // THE PRAYING HANDS

"*Legend has it that during the 1500's, in a tiny village near Nuremberg lived a family with eighteen children. To keep food on the table, the father, a goldsmith by profession, worked almost 16 hours a day at his trade and any other paying chore he could find in his neighborhood. Despite their seemingly hopeless condition, two of the children had a dream. They both wanted to pursue their talent for art, but they knew that their father would never be financially able to send either of them to Nuremberg to study at the academy. After many discussions, the 2 boys finally worked out a pact. They would toss a coin. The loser would go down into the nearby mines, and with the earnings, support his brother while he attended the academy. Then, when that brother who won the toss completed his studies, he would support the other brother while he attended school.*

They tossed a coin and Albrecht won the toss and went off to Nuremberg.

The other brother, Albert, went down into the mines, and for the next 4 years financed his brother whose work at the academy was almost an immediate sensation. By the time he graduated, he was beginning to earn considerable fees for his artwork.

When he went to his village, the family held a festive dinner to celebrate his triumphant homecoming. After the meal, Albrecht rose to drink a toast to his beloved brother for the years of sacrifice that had enabled Albrecht to fulfill his ambition. His closing words were, "Albert, blessed brother of mine, it is your turn. Now you can go to Nuremberg to pursue your dream, and I will take care of you."

Albert rose and said softly, "No brother. I cannot go to Nuremberg. It is too late for me. Look what 4 years in the mines have done to my hands!! The bones in every finger have been smashed at least once, and lately, I have been suffering from arthritis so badly in my right hand that I cannot even hold a glass to return your toast, much less make delicate leaves with a pen of a brush. No, brother, for me it is too late.

More than 450 years passed. Now hundreds of Albrecht Durer's masterful portraits hang in every great museum in the world, but the odds are great that you, like most people, are familiar with only one of them. You very well may have a reproduction hanging in your home or office.

To pay homage to Albert for all that he had sacrificed, Albrecht Durer drew his brother's hands with palms together and fingers stretched skyward. He called his powerful drawing simply "Hands", but the world has renamed his tribute of love "The Praying Hands". It is a tribute to true friendship, a love that is willing to do whatever is required to see another succeed. ”[41]

John 15:13 (ESV)

This is the very best way to love. Put your life on the line for your friends.

1 Corinthians 15:33 (ESV)

Be not deceived: Evil communications corrupt good manners.

There are 4 main principles to master when flying airplanes.

Lift, Thrust, Weight, and Drag

You have to take all these into account to make sure the plane will fly.

There are 4 types of friends //

1. **Lifters** –
   Who brighten your day
   Cheer you up
   Make you feel better about yourself

2. **Thrusters** –
   Who inspire you
   Motivate you
   Challenge you to move forward

3. **Weights** –
   Pull you down
   Dump their problems on you
   Leave heavy

4. **Drags** –
   Always got a sad song
   Always in a pit

THINK ON IT //

1. Do you have good friends in your life?

2. What kind of friend are you?

Notes

19

FOCUS

DAY 19

FOCUS

//BIG THOUGHT//

The more you focus on what you want, the more you will get what you want.

Have you ever wondered why a lion tamer carries a stool with them when they enter the lion's cage? As I began to study this, what I found was very interesting. The lion tamer holds the stool and shoves the legs towards the face of the lion. This throws the lion off, because he doesn't know where to focus and tries to focus on all four legs at the same time. In the attempt to focus on all four stool legs, a kind of paralysis happens and the lion becomes confused.

I've found that this is also the way it can be when it comes to focus. You go to church and are inspired to be bold as a lion, and it ignites your faith, but then church is over and life hits you. Circumstances are like a four-legged stool – maybe it's a relationship, school, job, or something else that distracts you, and you lose focus. That is exactly what the enemy wants, because once you lose focus, you lose where you are going in life.

Hebrews 12:1-4 (ESV)

Therefore, since we are surrounded by so great a cloud of witnesses, let us also lay aside every weight, and sin which clings so closely, and let us run with endurance the race that is set before us looking to Jesus, the founder and perfecter of our faith, who for the joy that was set before Him endured the cross, despising the shame, and is seated at the right hand of the throne of God. Consider Him who endured from sinners such hostility against himself, so that you may not grow weary or fainthearted. In your struggle against sin you have not yet resisted to the point of shedding your blood.

Paul encourages the Hebrew believer to keep focused on Christ and in life. It is very important that believers keep the proper focus in life. Whatever has your focus has your attention, whatever has your attention has your focus.

STORY //

> "*A hungry tiger started tracking the scent of a deer. As he followed the deer, he came across the scent of a rabbit. He turned aside and started after the rabbit. Then he was distracted by the scent of a mouse and started following that. He finally came to the hole into which the mouse had vanished. He ended the day hungrier than when he had started the day.*" [42]

This fable illustrates how many spend their lives distracted with this or that, and at the end of the day they have accomplished little. Stay on target; stay focused! Nothing is as important as following Jesus.

How to stay focused on Jesus:

1. **Spend time with God every day by praying and talking to Him.**

2. **Reading His Word every day.**

3. **Time in worship, being in His presence.**

4. **Hanging with people who are focused on Jesus like you are focused on Jesus.**

Follow
One
Course
Until
Successful

Focus on where you want to be, not where you were, or where you are!

> *"The successful warrior is the average man, with laser-like focus."* – Bruce Lee [43]

"You must remain focused on your journey to greatness." – Les Brown [44]

1 Corinthians 9:24-27 (ESV) -
Do you not know that in a race all the runners run, but only one receives the prize? So, run that you may obtain it. Every athlete exercises self-control in all things. They do it to receive a perishable wreath, but we an imperishable. So, I do not run aimlessly; I do not box as one beating the air. But I discipline my body and keep it under control, lest after preaching to others I myself should be disqualified.

TAKE A LOOK DEEPER //

Proverbs 4:25 (ESV) -
Let your eyes look directly forward, and your gaze be straight before you.

Proverbs 16:3 (ESV) -
Commit your work to the Lord, and your plans will be established.

Colossians 3:2 (ESV) -
Set your minds on things that are above, not on things that are on earth.

When athletes run a race, they use self-control and focus. They focus on running the race; the runner has a goal, a purpose. That purpose is to finish the race they began. If a runner can have that much focus and determination, how much more should we as believers in Christ who run for an eternal crown have? Discipline yourself, much like the athlete needs to, through self-control and focus.

The most powerful thing that someone can control is their focus. Focus determines everything in life. It has the power to help you determine what you see and what you accomplish in life. Without laser focus, you would be like a roller coaster with the ups and downs and twists and turns. Focus plays a big role in the life of a Christian. If the enemy gets the believer distracted, He wins. It is like shooting a powerful rifle, there are three steps – ready, aim, and fire. Ready means that you are spiritually focused on where you are going. Aim means that you see it in your view. You are not there yet, but you have a target. Fire means you have the passion and enthusiasm to stay focused and hit the target.

THINK ON IT

1. Are you ready to focus?

2. What are you aiming for?

3. Once you know what your target is, get ready to fire and accomplish that goal!

Notes

20

PRAYER

DAY 20

PRAYER

//BIG THOUGHT//

"Prayer is simply a two-way conversation between you and God."

- Billy Graham [45]

James 5:16 (ESV) -

...The prayer of a righteous person has great power as it is working.

Prayer is us staying connected with God and God staying connected with us. Every day we need to be communicating with God through prayer. Prayers are having a basic conversation with our Heavenly Father.

STORY //

> *"A man who worked as a messenger for a photo lab got a message instructing him to pick up a package at an unfamiliar company with a long, difficult name. He looked skyward and exclaimed, "God, where am I supposed to go?" Just then, he received another message, this time with the client's exact address. A man nearby witnessed this scene. Raising his arms to the heavens, he cried, "Why don't you ever answer me?""* [46]

Do you ever wish that prayer worked like that? You pray and instantly a voice gives you the answer you're looking for! Sign me up! But I find prayer to be a much more difficult process. I need all the help I can get on how to pray more effectively.

Psalm 145:18 (ESV) -

The Lord is near to all who call on Him, to all who call on Him in truth.

See, God is always there and is always listening. Don't ever feel like God isn't listening to you. When you begin to think that way, your faith in Him is weakened. Don't ever feel like God is not concerned about your prayers or your cries. He is concerned about everything. When you pray, He hears you.

Matthew 7:7 (ESV) -

Ask, and it will be given to you; seek, and you will find; knock, and it will be opened to you.

You have to seek the Lord, and the Lord will answer your prayers. He is waiting for you to seek Him and spend time in His presence. He wants your attention.

STORY //

"There was a sweet grandma who had two grandsons, who were always getting in trouble, hanging with the wrong crowd, and making wrong decisions which led them to doing the wrong things. One day the teenagers got in so much trouble, that they stood before a judge, and the judge gave them two choices. One, they could go into the military, or two, they could go to jail. Both of them decided to go into the military. The grandma continued to pray for her grandsons. For fourteen years, she prayed that God would save them. Sometimes her faith became weak, but she kept praying and believing. As her two grandsons were in the navy, they found themselves on leave in the Philippines for two days. One night they heard music and assumed there was a party. It was actually a missionary performing a Christian concert as an outreach. As the two young sailors listened to the music, they heard the message. That evening, on an island in the Philippines, they responded to the Gospel and gave their lives to Christ. They wrote their grandma a postcard telling her that they had made a decision to give their life to Jesus and to serve Him. They told her about this great man of God who was an evangelist and lead them in the sinner's prayer. As the grandma read the postcard, she began to tear up. Not only did her grandsons find the Lord, but also, she realized that she had been financially supporting this missionary evangelist for fourteen years."

Isn't that a powerful story? See, God DOES answer prayers! In fact, in His Word He gives you an example of how you are to pray.

Matthew 6:9-13, ESV (The Lord's Prayer) - *Pray then like this: "Our Father in heaven, hallowed be Your name. Your kingdom come, Your will be done, on earth as it is in heaven. Give us this day our daily bread, and forgive us our debts, as we also have forgiven our debtors. And lead us not into temptation, but deliver us from evil.*

I love this prayer, The Lord's Prayer. It is a wonderful outline to use for your personal prayer life. God is your Heavenly Father. His will is going to be done. His will is perfect. He forgives us, and you need to forgive those who have hurt you or done wrong by you. God doesn't tempt you, but He makes a way for you to escape temptation and wrong. It's important to understand that prayer is easy. The more you pray, the better you get at praying. You can pray anywhere and everywhere. Believe in the power of prayer; because prayer changes lives, it changes circumstances, it makes impossible situations possible, and it gives hope to the hopeless and brokenhearted.

THINK ON IT

Take a few minutes to pray (talk) to God. He is waiting to hear from you. Something that I have told people for years is to set an empty 7-Up bottle next to their bed, and let it be a reminder that when they wake up in the morning to give God the first seven minutes of their day.

____

____

____

____

____

21

EVANGELISM

DAY 21

EVANGELISM

//BIG THOUGHT//

Evangelism is sharing the gospel with every person. Sharing the Gospel of Jesus Christ should not be optional for the believer.

What is Evangelism?

Evangelism is spreading the gospel message of Jesus Christ. It is zealously sharing the love of God with others. Jesus gave us a commandment in Matthew and Mark to go into all the world and preach the gospel.

Matthew 28:16-20 (ESV)

Now the eleven disciples went to Galilee, to the mountain to which Jesus had directed them. And when they saw him they worshiped him, but some doubted. And Jesus came and said to them, "All authority in heaven and on earth has been given to me. Go therefore and make disciples of all nations, baptizing them in the name of the Father and of the Son and of the Holy Spirit, teaching them to observe all that I have commanded you. And behold, I am with you always, to the end of the age."

Mark 16:15 (ESV)

And he said to them, "Go into all the world and proclaim the gospel to the whole creation.

In the Great Commission, we are commanded by Jesus to go into all the world and preach the gospel, the Good News to the lost and hurting people. So, what is that Good News? The Good News is that God loved us so much that He gave His only son for us so that we could be reconciled to Him.

John 3:16 (ESV)

For God so loved the world, that he gave his only Son, that whoever believes in him should not perish but have eternal life.

It's that simple! God has called us to share Jesus with the world!

Three major points that we see in John 3:16 are:

1. **The Giver: God**
   God is the ultimate giver, who gave us the greatest gift ever- Jesus!

2. **The Gift: Jesus**
   Jesus is the greatest gift ever given to mankind!

3. **The Guarantee: Eternal Life**
   If we accept the amazing gift of Jesus from the ultimate giver, God, then we are guaranteed eternal life with Him in heaven!

STORY // The Painting

"*A wealthy man and his son loved to collect rare works of art. They had everything in their collection, from Picasso to Raphael. They would often sit together and admire the great works of art. When the Vietnam conflict broke out, the son went to war. He was very courageous and died in battle while rescuing another soldier.*

The father was notified and grieved deeply for his only son. About a month later, just before Christmas, there was a knock at the door. A young man stood at the door with a large package in his hands. He said, "Sir, you don't know me, but I am the soldier for whom your son gave his life. He saved many lives that day, and he was carrying me to safety when a bullet struck him in the heart, and he died instantly. He often talked about you, and your love for art."

The young man held out his package. "I know this isn't much. I'm not really a great artist, but I think your son would have wanted you to have this."

The father unwrapped the package. It was a portrait of his son, painted by the young man. He stared in awe at the way the soldier had captured the personality of his son in the painting. The father was so drawn to the eyes that his own eyes welled up with tears. He thanked the young man and offered to pay him for the picture.

"Oh, no sir." Said the soldier. "I could never repay what your son did for me. It's a gift."

The father hung the portrait over his mantle. Every time visitors came to his home he took them to see the portrait of his son before he showed them any of the other great works he had collected.

The man died a few months later. There was to be a great auction of his paintings. Many influential people gathered, excited over seeing the great paintings and getting an opportunity to purchase one for their collection. On the platform sat the painting of the son.

The auctioneer pounded his gravel. "We will start bidding with this picture of the son.

There was silence.

Then a voice in the back of the room shouted, "We want to see the famous paintings. Skip this one."

But the auctioneer persisted, "Will someone bid for this painting? Who will start the bidding? $100, $200?

Another voice shouted angrily, "We didn't come to see this painting. We came to see the Van Gogh's, the Rembrandts. Get on with the real bids!"

But the auctioneer continued, "The son! The son! Who'll take the son?"

Finally, a voice came from the very back of the room. It was the longtime gardener of the man and his son. "I'll give $10 for the painting."

Being a poor man, it was all he could afford.

"We have $10, who will bid $20?

"Give it to him for $10. Let's see the masters."

"$10 Is the bid, won't someone bid $20?

The crowd was becoming angry. They didn't want the picture of the son. They wanted the worthier investments for their collections.

The auctioneer pounded the gavel. "Going once, twice, SOLD for $10!"

A man sitting on the second row shouted, "Now let's get on with the collection!"

The auctioneer laid down his gavel, "I'm sorry, the auction is over."

"What about the paintings?"

"I am sorry. When I was called to conduct this auction, I was told a secret stipulation in the will. I was not allowed to reveal that stipulation until this time. Only the painting of the son would be auctioned. Whoever bought that painting would inherit the entire estate, including the paintings. The man who took the son gets everything!" ” [47]

This is the very story that the world needs to know. God is looking for us to share our faith with people who are hurting and desperate. God wants us to bring the gift of Jesus, His Son, to those who need to hear the truth of God's amazing love for them. As a Christian, a believer of Jesus Christ, a follower of the Master, we are called to bring hope into people's lives. It is our responsibility. God has given each of us a unique identity and story, so we can minister to those who will listen.

The idea of sharing your faith can be scary, but in reality, it is very easy. All you are doing is sharing the love of God with someone else. No one will ever love someone the way God loves them. An incredible guideline to use when sharing the love of God with someone is the Romans Road.

//The Romans Road //

- » Romans 3:10
- » Romans 3:23
- » Romans 5:8
- » Romans 6:23
- » Romans 10:9-10
- » Romans 10:13
- » Romans 12:1

STORY // The Rich Young Man
(Matthew 19:16-22, ESV)

> "*And behold, a man came up to him, saying, "Teacher, what good deed must I do to have eternal life?" And he said to him, "Why do you ask me about what is good? There is only one who is good. If you would enter life, keep the commandments." He said to him, "Which ones?" And Jesus said, "You shall not murder, You shall not commit adultery, You shall not steal, You shall not bear false witness, Honor your father and mother, and, You shall love your neighbor as yourself." The young man said to him, "All these I have kept. What do I still lack?" Jesus said to him, "If you would be perfect, go, sell what you possess and give to the poor, and you will have treasure in heaven; and come, follow me." When the young man heard this he went away sorrowful, for he had great possessions.*"

In this story, we see a rich young man asking what he needs to do to obtain eternal life. In verse 16, Jesus answers him, telling him to keep the commandments. The young man, filled with a lot of pride, tells Jesus he has obeyed all of them since he was a child. Jesus told him if he wanted eternal life, then to go and sell all he had. This was a test to see what was the most important thing in his heart, and we find out that it was his possessions. In verse 21, Jesus said three of the most powerful words - "Come, follow Me." Then in the very next verse we see three of the saddest words, "he walked away." The rich young man wasn't willing to give up all that he had to follow Jesus. His stuff, his worldly possessions, were more important to him then following Jesus, the Master and Creator of the universe. That is so true with so many people in this world. They hear the Gospel, sometimes they can even see the goodness of God, yet they walk away and decide not to follow Him.

THINK ON IT

Jesus commands us to share the Gospel with the lost and to live in such a way that people would be drawn to us, because they see Jesus in us. Are you living in a way that others can see Jesus in you? If you hesitated at all in answering this question, what are things you need to change so that Jesus shines in your life?

Notes

22

WHAT IF?

DAY 22

WHAT IF?

//BIG THOUGHT//
If success was guaranteed, and failure wasn't an option, what would you desire to do?

> *Definition of What if:*
> *A suggestion, proposal, a speculation as to what might happen.*

These two words can be powerful. They can engage the imagination to see greater things or stir up fear and doubt. They can help us to see things outside the box, or try to keep people inside the box. What if implies possibility or even wonder.

What if?

What if you couldn't lose?
What if no one could stop you?
What if all you did was win?

Will the "what if" break you or make you stronger? God made you to win, but you have to see yourself that way.

The What If?

- What if there was a movement that brought the world to Jesus?
- What if the impossible was possible?
- What if our fears became faith?
- What if our dreams came true?
- What if you gave God your everything?
- What if God really loved you more than you know?

What are your dreams? What do you want to do? Every day is a new beginning and an opportunity to stay away from what might have been and look at…"What can be". Ask yourself this question, what if I can make a difference? Most people are afraid. Most people today never really expect to make a difference in anything, so they give up. All we have is now!

"Opportunity is missed by most people because it comes dressed in overalls and looks like work."
- Thomas Edison [48]

I think Edison was right. People often do shy away from things that require some effort. There will be times in life that things don't go as you want them to. That is when you have to remember that God is by your side and will help to guide and direct you through it.

Remember this -

You will never make a positive difference for Christ with a critical, negative spirit.

Someone once said,

"There is little growth on the mountaintop. Growth occurs in the valley. Everybody wants to be on the mountaintop, but the view is in the valley."

Our best growth doesn't take place in the mountaintop experiences of life, but growth takes place in the valleys. No pain, no gain!

"A successful person is one who gets up one more time than he is knocked down." - Paul Harvey

"If you act the way you wish you felt, you will eventually feel the way you act." - William James

Take a look at this story of Paul and Silas that is found in **Acts 16:16-34 (ESV)**.

> *As we were going to the place of prayer, we were met by a slave girl who had a spirit of divination and brought her owners much gain by fortune-telling. She followed Paul and us, crying out, "These men are servants of the Most High God, who proclaim to you the way of salvation." And this she kept doing for many days. Paul, having become greatly annoyed, turned and said to the spirit, "I command you in the name of Jesus Christ to come out of her." And it came out that very hour. But when her owners saw that their hope of gain was gone, they seized Paul and Silas and dragged them into the marketplace before the rulers. And when they had brought them to the magistrates, they said, "These men are Jews, and they are disturbing our city. They advocate customs that are not lawful for us as Romans to accept or practice." The crowd joined in attacking them, and the magistrates tore the garments off them and gave orders to beat them with rods. And when they had inflicted many blows upon them, they threw them into prison, ordering the jailer to keep them safely. Having received this order, he put them into the inner prison and fastened their feet in the stocks. About midnight Paul and Silas were praying and singing hymns to God, and the prisoners were listening to them, and suddenly there was a great earthquake, so that the foundations of the prison were shaken. And immediately all the doors were opened, and everyone's bonds were unfastened. When the jailer woke and saw that the prison doors were open, he drew his sword and was about to kill himself, supposing that the prisoners had es-*

caped. But Paul cried with a loud voice, "Do not harm yourself, for we are all here." And the jailer called for lights and rushed in, and trembling with fear he fell down before Paul and Silas. Then he brought them out and said, "Sirs, what must I do to be saved?" And they said, "Believe in the Lord Jesus, and you will be saved, you and your household." And they spoke the word of the Lord to him and to all who were in his house. And he took them the same hour of the night and washed their wounds; and he was baptized at once, he and all his family. Then he brought them up into his house and set food before them. And he rejoiced along with his entire household that he had believed in God.

Paul had to ask himself, what if it's about more than the earthquake? What if it's about something else instead? What if the earthquake wasn't so much about Paul's freedom as it was for the jailer to be free? So many times, we don't believe the what if God could do a miracle. Here is a story of God setting men free physically and spiritually. If you have a what if belief that God CAN, then by faith it can be done.

In order for your what if to work, you need to -

1. **Believe in Jesus**

2. **Believe in yourself**

3. **Be sold out to the Gospel**

Be sold out to that what if you want for your life! Your destiny requires your discipline. When people ask me, what do you do when? I say: "Whatever it takes!" Be that "whatever it takes" person. The possibilities are endless with God. Don't limit Him!

THINK ON IT

Are You A…

1. Hold out
   A hold out is someone who holds out for something better and misses the very opportunity that is in front of him/her.

2. Drop out
   A drop out is someone who seizes the opportunity, but does not follow through with it.

3. Sold out
   A sold out is someone who takes the what if approach and gives it everything he has to see it through to the end.

23

IDENTITY

DAY 23

IDENTITY

//BIG THOUGHT//

People with healthy self-esteems don't need to crate pretend identities.

– Bell Hooks [49]

> *Definition of Identity:*
> *The fact of being who or what a person or thing is, and the qualities, beliefs, etc. that makes a particular person or group different from others.* [50]

Have you ever asked yourself, who am I? You are a son or daughter of the Most High God! The Bible says in Genesis 1:27 that we are made (created) in the image of God. In God is where you find your true identity!

1. **You were created in God's image!**

Genesis 1:26-27 (ESV) -

Then God said, "Let us make man in our image, after our likeness. And let them have dominion over the fish of the sea and over the birds of the heavens and over the livestock and over all the earth and over every creeping thing that creeps on the earth. So, God created man in His own image, in the image of God He created him; male and female He created them.

God has designed you in His image and has given you dominion over every living thing! You have been made and are destined for greatness! You are made in His likeness, and that means that you are to imitate Him and not anyone else.

Psalm 8:3-6 (ESV) -
When I look at Your heavens, the work of Your fingers, the moon and the stars, which You have set in place, what is man that you are mindful of him, and the son of man that you care for him? Yet you have made him a little lower than the heavenly beings and crowned him with glory and honor. You have given him dominion over the works of Your hands; You have put all things under his feet.

2. **You are unique.**

You have been fearfully and wonderfully made by God.

Psalm 139:14 (ESV) -
I praise you, for I am fearfully and wonderfully made.

You are God's handiwork. **(Ephesians 2:10)**
You are complete in God's eyes. **(Colossians 2:10)**
You are forgiven and redeemed in God's eyes. **(Ephesians 1:7)**
You are the salt and light of the world in God's eyes. **(Matthew 5:13-14)**

"You have a fingerprint that no one else has, to leave an imprint in this world that no one else can leave! Your unique and one-of-a-kind fingerprint gives you the power to make an impact and leave an imprint on the people that you come into contact with."
– Pastor Keith Craft, Leadershipology.com [51]

"Man was designed for accomplishment, engineered for success and endowed with seeds of greatness."
– Zig Ziglar [52]

> *"God can't bless who you pretend to be."*
> – Steven Furtick [53]

STORY // Shadrach, Meshach, Abednego
(Daniel 3:24-30, ESV)

"During the rule of King Nebuchadnezzar, the people of Babylon worshipped many false gods. The king made a large gold statue and established a decree requiring all people to publicly bow down and worship the statue. There were three young Hebrew men living in Babylon during the reign of Nebuchadnezzar, Shadrach, Meshach, and Abednego. They worshipped the one true God and refused to bow to the gold statue the king had made.

The men were brought before the King, and told him they served the Almighty God and would not worship the king's false gods and statues, knowing that the punishment for this was death. King Nebuchadnezzar was furious. He ordered the men to be thrown into the fiery furnace, but God has another plan. The men were tied and thrown into the furnace. Look what happened!

Then King Nebuchadnezzar was astonished and rose up in haste. He declared to his counselors, "Did we not cast three men bound into the fire?" They answered and said to the king, "True, O king." He answered and said, "But I see four men unbound, walking in the midst of the fire, and they are not hurt; and the appearance of the fourth is like a son of the gods." Then Nebuchadnezzar came near to the door of the burning fiery furnace; he declared, "Shadrach, Meshach, and Abednego, servants of the Most High God, come out, and come here!" Then Shadrach, Meshach, and Abednego came out from the fire. And the satraps, the prefects, the governors, and the king's counselors gathered together and saw that the fire had not had any power over the bodies of those men. The hair of their heads was not singed, their cloaks were not harmed, and no smell of fire had come upon them. Nebuchadnezzar answered and said, "Blessed be the God of Shadrach, Meshach, and Abednego, who has sent his angel and delivered his servants, who trusted in him, and set aside the king's command, and yielded up their bodies rather than serve and worship any god except their own God. Therefore, I make a decree: Any people, nation, or language that speaks anything against the God of Shadrach, Meshach, and Abednego shall be torn limb from limb, and their houses laid in ruins, for there is no other god who is able to rescue in this way." Then the king promoted Shadrach, Meshach, and Abednego in the province of Babylon."

The men were able to make that stand, because they knew who they were in God. They spent time with God. They trusted that God would save them, and He did! Know who you are and find your identity in God, just like Shadrach, Meshach, and Abednego did!

THINK ON IT

1. Do you worry about what people think about you? If so, find out what God says about you by digging deeper in His Word.

Notes

Notes

24

TRUST

DAY 24

TRUST

//BIG THOUGHT//

A relationship without trust is like a car without gas; you can stay in it all you want, but it won't go anywhere.

Definition of Trust:
To depend on the strength or ability of a person or thing. [54]

You know, many people put their trust in a lot of different things, people, money, fame, friendship, and the list can keep going. We should trust God with everything we got. God is for you; He loves you. God can be trusted; He will never disappoint you. Think about this, every day we put our trust in people and things. You trust every day, even if you don't think about it.

Proverbs 3:5-6 (ESV) -

Trust in the Lord with all your heart, and do not lean on your own understanding. In all your ways acknowledge him, and he will make straight your paths.

This is a major verse for your life. It is a reminder of what you should do when you are lacking trust. You need to put your trust in the Lord every day, and every day trust in the Lord. Life's struggles and difficulties will always be better when you put your trust in the Lord.

STORY // Bethany Hamilton
(Found on www.soulsurfer.com)

"*It came, literally, out of the blue. I had no warning at all, not even the slightest hint of danger on the horizon. The waves were small and inconsistent, and I was just kind of rolling along with them, relaxing on my board with my left arm dangling in the cool water. I remember thinking, "I hope the surf picks up soon..."*

That's all it took: a split second. I felt a lot of pressure and a couple of lightning fast tugs. Then I watched in shock as the water around me turned bright red. Somehow, I stayed calm. My left arm was gone almost to the armpit, along with a huge crescent-shaped chunk on my red, white and blue surfboard...

I remember most clearly what the Kauai paramedic said to me in the ambulance: He spoke softly and held my hand as we were pulling out of the beach parking lot. He whispered in my ear, "God will never leave you or forsake you." He was right.

I believe in God. Nobody made me believe; I don't think you can or should try to force someone to believe something. And even though my parents taught me stuff about God and read Bible stories to me from as early as I can remember... it was my choice to become a believer in Him. The way I see it, putting our faith in God is something that each person has to come to on his or her own. It's your own personal relationship with Him; a bond that's as unique as a fingerprint." [55]

The most expensive thing in the world is trust. For every set back, God has a major come back, Trust Him! Let's take a look at Daniel and see how God came through for him.

STORY // Daniel and the Lion's Den
(Daniel 6, ESV)

"*This is a story of a man who was passionate about seeking God. He knew that even though it was against the law to pray to anyone other than the King, he openly prayed to the one true God three times a day. When the rulers of the kingdom saw Daniel breaking the law, they reported him to the King and demanded a punishment. The King ordered Daniel to be thrown into the den of lions. God sent angels to shut the mouths of the lions and delivered Daniel. Daniel put his trust in the Lord.*"

Jeremiah 17:7 (ESV) -

Blessed is the man who trusts in the Lord,
whose trust is the Lord.

THINK ON IT

Do you put your trust in the Lord? He wants you to trust Him fully and completely. Has He ever given you a reason not to? Of course not! God is a loving, caring God who has a plan and purpose for your life. Trust Him with it.

25

PASSION

DAY 25

PASSION

//BIG THOUGHT//

People with great passion can make the impossible happen.

Passion is the dividing factor between success and failure.

French military strategist, Ferdinand Foch said, “The most powerful weapon on earth is the human soul on fire.” [56] Helen Keller once said, “Life is either a daring adventure or it’s nothing.” [57] Passion gives you the enthusiasm to live a life worth living. Passion on the inside affects everything on the outside. Be determined to live a life that matters. Make a difference and change the world you live in, because you are a world-changer.

> *"Nothing great in the world has been accomplished without passion."*
> - George Wihelm Fredrick Hegel, German philosopher [58]

> *"Enthusiasm and persistence can make an average person superior; indifference and lethargy can make a superior person average."* - William Ward [59]

Romans 12:11 (ESV) -

Do not be slothful in zeal, be fervent in spirit, serve the Lord.

Zeal is another word for passion. God wants Christians to be passionate in their heart about – Him, the Church, life, family, friends, dreams, work, goals, hobbies; He wants His children to live a life full of passion (fire, zeal). Passion and purpose always go together. A follower of Jesus without passion is like a river without water. You should always be looking to increase your passion for God. You should associate with people of passion, and people who encourage and inspire you.

Hebrews 10:24-25 (ESV) -

And let us consider how to stir up one another to love and good works, not neglecting to meet together, as is the habit of some, but encouraging one another, and all the more as you see the Day drawing near.

There is a tale told of that great English actor Macready. An eminent preacher once said to him:

> "*I wish you would explain to me something. Well, what is it? I don't know that I can explain anything to a preacher.*"
>
> *"What is the reason for the difference between you and I? You are appearing before crowd's night after night with fiction, and the crowds come wherever you go. I am preaching the essential and unchangeable truth, and I am not getting any crowd at all."*
>
> *Macready's answer was this:*
>
> *"This is quite simple. I can tell you the difference between us. I present fiction as though it were truth; you present your truth as though it were fiction."* " [60]

Do it with passion, or don't do it at all. Passion is the game-changer in life.

STORY // Circus Lion vs. Jungle Lion

> "*The strength of the lion tamer does not lie in the fact that he is stronger than the lion, but that the lion thinks he is. Although the lion is the most ferocious animal in the jungle, it will sit, roll over, and play dead at the crack of the tamer's whip. The lion tamer would not dare go into the jungle and ask to see the great king. The difference between the two is that the circus lion has been stripped of the knowledge of its greatness.*"

The strength of our adversaries does not lie in the fact that they are stronger than we are, but that we think they are. Don't let the devil strip you of the destiny that God has for you.

STORY // Peter Heals the Lame Man
(Acts 3:1-16, ESV)

> *"Now Peter and John were going up to the temple at the hour of prayer, the ninth hour. And a man lame from birth was being carried, whom they laid daily at the gate of the temple that is called the Beautiful Gate to ask alms of those entering the temple. Seeing Peter and John about to go into the temple, he asked to receive alms. And Peter directed his gaze at him, as did John, and said, "Look at us." And he fixed his attention on them, expecting to receive something from them. But Peter said, "I have no silver and gold, but what I do have I give to you. In the name of Jesus Christ of Nazareth, rise up and walk!" And he took him by the right hand and raised him up, and immediately his feet and ankles were made strong. And leaping up, he stood and began to walk, and entered the temple with them, walking and leaping and praising God. And all the people saw him walking and praising God, and recognized him as the one who sat at the Beautiful Gate of the temple, asking for alms. And they were filled with wonder and amazement at what had happened to him. While he clung to Peter and John, all the people, utterly astounded, ran together to them in the portico called Solomon's. And when Peter saw it he addressed the people: "Men of Israel, why do you wonder at this, or why do you stare at us, as though by our own power or piety we have made him walk? The God of Abraham, the God of Isaac, and the God of Jacob, the God of our fathers, glorified his servant Jesus, whom you delivered over and denied in the presence of Pilate, when he had decided to release him. But you denied the Holy and Righteous One, and asked for a murderer to be granted to you, and you killed the Author of life, whom God raised from the dead. To this we are witnesses. And his name—by faith in his name—has made this man strong whom you see and know, and the faith that is through Jesus has given the man this perfect health in the presence of you all."*

Peter and John were filled with passion to serve the Lord. Their passion caused them to react when they saw the beggar. Their passion for God is what caused them to stop, step up and step out and pray for the beggar to be healed. Passionate people do amazing things. Commit today to be more passionate for God!

THINK ON IT

1. Are you passionate about serving the Lord?

2. Take a moment to list some things that you are passionate about.

Notes

26

COURAGE

DAY 26

COURAGE

//BIG THOUGHT//

Courage is not having the strength to go on. It is going on when you don't have the strength.

Courage is doing what you're afraid to do. Courage is stepping up when no one else does. Courage is making the hard decisions. When you have courage, you will win!

STORY //Last Stand

> *"Leonidas, King of Sparta, was preparing to make a stand with his Greek troops against the Persian army in 480 B.C when a Persian envoy arrived. The man urged Leonidas on the futility of trying to resist the advance of the huge Persian army. "Our archers are so numerous," said the envoy "that the flight of their arrows darkens the sun." "So much the better," replied Leonidas. "For we shall fight them in the shade." Leonidas made his stand."* [61]

What do you say in the midst of fear or worry? Courage is not having all the answers, but trusting in God for He has all the answers. With God's protection and guidance, you should be able to conquer fears and live a life full of courage. It is God that commands us to have courage, for having courage means having faith and confidence in Him.

//TAKE A LOOK //

Ephesians 6:10 (ESV) -

Finally, be strong in the Lord and in the strength of His might.

Deuteronomy 31:6 (ESV) -

Be strong and courageous. Do not fear or be in dread of them, for it is the Lord your God who goes with you. He will not leave you or forsake you.

Psalm 27:1 (ESV) -
The Lord is my light and my salvation; whom shall I fear? The Lord is the stronghold of my life; of whom shall I be afraid?

2 Timothy 1:7 (ESV) -
For God gave us a spirit not of fear but of power and love and self-control.

Joshua 1:9 (ESV) -
Have I not commanded you? Be strong and courageous. Do not be frightened, and do not be dismayed, for the Lord your God is with you wherever you go.

Psalm 31:24 (ESV) -
Be strong, and let your heart take courage, all you who wait for the Lord!

There are so many verses in the Bible that talk about having courage and not being afraid. God is for you; He is on your side. Be confident in what His Word says. He tells you to be strong, to be courageous, and to not fear. God will never leave you or forsake you!

STORY // David and Goliath
(1 Samuel 17:1-54, ESV)

> *"David was a teenager who showed up to a battle, because he was told to bring his older brothers some food. When David heard the Philistine giant, Goliath, insulting God and the people of Israel, he didn't just stand by, he had courage, and got ready for the battle with Goliath. He put his faith and courage in God; he knew that God was with him and not going to leave him, and God gave David and the army of Israel victory!"*

Courage will follow when faith takes the lead!

A ship is always safe at shore but that is not what it's built for.
– Albert Einstein [62]

Were you ever afraid of the dark? You know, you're lying in bed when all of a sudden you see a shadow moving by your opened closet door. You quickly sit up and pull the blankets close. The shadow moves a little bit more. Your heart beats fast as you stare into the dark void. Something terrible must be inside. How can you possibly sleep with such a terrifying and dangerous beast lurking in your closet? You only have one option. In a sudden burst of courage, you jump from the bed and run to the light switch. When the light enters the room you cautiously look to the dreaded closet. What you see shocks you. It was a box of stuffed animals with an old pair of shorts thrown over the top. Your fear was based on a lifeless object but your courage caused you to overcome and conquer your fear.

Courage doesn't mean you don't get afraid at times, it means you don't let it stop you. God has big plans for your life. Don't stop going forward.

Romans 8:37 (ESV) -
"No, in all these things we are more than conquerors through him who loved us."

With God, you have the victory, so be courageous! Don't let anything stop you from what God speaks to your heart.

3 Reasons to Take Courage in Your Life //

1. **God made you! (Psalm 139:14, ESV)**
2. **God is for you! (Romans 8:31, ESV)**
3. **God is with you! (Isaiah 41:10, ESV)**

THINK ON IT

Whatever you do in life, you will need courage. Whatever course you decide, you will need courage. Whatever dream you want to achieve, you will need courage.

Notes

Notes

27

LOVE

DAY 27

LOVE

//BIG THOUGHT//

It is not how much you do, but how much love you put into what you do that counts. – Mother Teresa [63]

Love is one powerful 4 letter word! We love others best when we love God most. Love is everything as a follower of Jesus.

> *Definition of Love:*
> *Unselfish loyal and benevolent concern for the good of another; the object of devotion, or admiration.* [64]

Matthew 22:37 (ESV) -

And He said to him, "You shall love the Lord your God with all your heart and with all your soul and with all your mind."

Loving God with your whole heart helps you to love others better. If you can't love God, you will find it very hard to love others, maybe not at first, but to continue to have an unconditional love will not be easy.

John 4:7-10 (ESV) -

A woman from Samaria came to draw water. Jesus said to her, "Give me a drink." (For his disciples had gone away into the city to buy food.) The Samaritan woman said to him, "How is it that you, a Jew, ask for a drink from me, a woman of Samaria?" (For Jews have no dealings with Samaritans.) Jesus answered her, "If you knew the gift of God, and who it is that is saying to you, 'Give me a drink,' you would have asked him, and he would have given you living water."

Unconditional love only comes from God, and the love God offers is the only thing that can truly fill the void in our lives. God's love - you can't earn it, buy it, or win it. His love isn't conditional; His love isn't based on what you do. God's love for you is never ending. When it comes to God, you can be yourself. He loves you just the way you are! There is wholeness for you in God's love. You don't have to be something that you are not or be someone that you are not in order for God to love you. There is nothing like the love of God. It is the most overwhelming thing that you will ever experience in your life! God's love is unconditional, unchangeable, and unending.

John 15:13 (ESV) -
Greater love has no one than this, that someone lay down his life for his friends.

STORY // John Griffith, The Bridge Operator

It's a story that takes place in the 1920's in Oklahoma:

"John Griffith was in his early twenties. He was newly married and full of optimism. Along with his lovely wife, he had been blessed with a beautiful baby. He was living the American dream, but then came 1929 - the Great Stock Market Crash - the shattering of the American economy that devastated John's dreams. Brokenhearted, John packed up his few possessions, and with his wife and his little son, headed East in an old Ford Model A. They made their way to the edge of the mighty Mississippi River and found a job tending one of the great railroad bridges there.

Day after day, John would sit in the control room and direct the enormous gears of the immense bridge over the mighty river. He would look out wistfully as bulky barges and splendid ships glided gracefully under his elevated bridge. Each day, he looked on sadly as those ships carried with them his shattered dreams and his visions of far off places and exotic destinations.

It wasn't until 1937 that a new dream began to be birthed in John's heart. His young son was now eight years old, and John had begun to catch a vision for a new life, a life in which Greg, his little son, would work shoulder to shoulder with him. The first day of this new life dawned and brought with it new hope and fresh purpose. Excitedly, they packed their lunches and headed off towards the immense bridge. Greg looked on in wide-eyed amazement as his Dad pressed down the huge level that raised and lowered the vast bridge. As he watched, he thought that his father must surely be the greatest man alive. He marveled that his Dad could singlehandedly control the movements of such a stupendous structure. Before they knew it, noontime had arrived. John had just elevated the bridge and allowed some scheduled ships to pass through, and then, taking his son by the hand, they headed off to the observation deck for lunch.

As they ate, John told his son in vivid detail stories about the marvelous destinations of the ships that glided below them. Then, suddenly, in the midst of telling a tale about the time that the river had overflowed its banks, he and his son were startled back to reality by the shrieking whistle of a distant train, the Memphis Express, roaring toward the crossing. Looking at his watch in disbelief, he knew the bridge needed to be lowered. He told his son to stay put while he ran back to the control room. Leaping from the observation deck, he ran to throw the control switch. Glancing down, his heart stopped! His son had fallen into the gears, trapping his leg in the cogs. Desperately he tried to devise a rescue plan, but there was no time. His son was down there—but there were four hundred passengers on the train! Griffin knew what he had to do. Burying his face in his arm, he pushed the master switch just in time to lower the bridge into place as the train thundered across. John Griffith lifted his tear-stained face and looked into the windows of the passing train. A businessman was reading the morning newspaper. A uniformed conductor was glancing nonchalantly as his large vest pocket watch. Ladies were already sipping their afternoon tea in the dining cars. A small boy, looking strangely like his own son, pushed a long thin spoon into a large dish of ice cream. Many of the passengers seemed to be engaged in idle conversation or careless laughter. No one even looked his way, no one even cast a glance at the giant gear box that housed the mangled remains of his hopes and his dreams. In anguish, he pounded the glass in the control room. He cried out "What's the matter with you people? Don't you know? Don't you care? Don't you know I've sacrificed my son for you? What's wrong with you?" No one answered. No one heard. No one even looked. Not one of them seemed to care. Then, as suddenly as it had happened, it was over. The train disappeared moving rapidly across the bridge and out over the horizon.

That day John Griffith sacrificed his son and saved 400 people. This story is just a small glimpse of what the Father did in sacrificing his son for the sins of the world. Unlike the Memphis Express, however, an express that caught John Griffith by surprise, God in His great love determined to sacrifice his Son so that we might live. God will never let us down, because His love is unconditional. God is love and nothing can compete with His love - no individual, nothing can ever replace the love of God." [65]

John 3:16 (NKJV) -

For God so loved the world, that He gave his only Son, that whoever believes in Him should not perish but have eternal life.

God's love is so passionate that He willingly gave His only son, so that you could experience His love. The best way to find love is to find God.

» God designed you.
» God created you.
» God blessed you.
» God heals you.
» God cares for you.
» God defends you.
» God forgives you.
» God loves you.

Remember, you are loved by God and nothing can take that away from you!

THINK ON IT

The way you show love to others is a reflection of your love for God. If you fail in loving others, you have missed the love of God. You cannot love others like Christ, without Christ.

1 Corinthians 13, (ESV) -

Love is patient and kind; love does not envy or boast; it is not arrogant or rude. It does not insist on its own way; it is not irritable or resentful; it does not rejoice at wrongdoing, but rejoices with the truth. Love bears all things, believes all things, hopes all things, endures all things. Love never ends.

Notes

28

OBEDIENCE

DAY 28

OBEDIENCE

//BIG THOUGHT//

"Obedience is the act of faith; disobedience is the result of unbelief."

- Edwin Lewis Cole [66]

There is a story in the Bible found in Luke 5:1-11 (ESV) where the disciples are out on the boat fishing. Let's take a look.

> *"On one occasion, while the crowd was pressing in on Him to hear the word of God, he was standing by the lake of Gennesaret, and He saw two boats by the lake, but the fishermen had gone out of them and were washing their nets. Getting into one of the boats, which was Simon's, he asked him to put out a little from the land. And He sat down and taught the people from the boat. And when he had finished speaking, he said to Simon, "Put out into the deep and let down your nets for a catch." And Simon answered, "Master, we toiled all night and took nothing! But at your word I will let down the nets." And when they had done this, they enclosed a large number of fish, and their nets were breaking. They signaled to their partners in the other boat to come and help them. And they came and filled both the boats, so that they began to sink. But when Simon Peter saw it, he fell down at Jesus' knees, saying, "Depart from me, for I am a sinful man, O Lord." For he and all who were with him were astonished at the catch of fish that they had taken, and so also were James and John, sons of Zebedee, who were partners with Simon. And Jesus said to Simon, "Do not be afraid; from now on you will be catching men." And when they had brought their boats to land, they left everything and followed him."*

From this passage of scripture, we can see in verse 5 the disciples fished all night and caught nothing. In verse 6, their nets began to break, and they asked for help. Jesus turned an empty boat into a full one. The breaking nets are the result of God's blessing in their lives, because they obeyed, God honored them and gave them more than their boat could hold. When we obey, it lights the way! Obedience always comes down to a choice. These men had the choice to obey what Jesus said, or to do their own thing. If they had done their own thing, they would have missed out on the blessing. As a result of Simon's obedience, they were blessed and experienced a miracle.

Obedience is better than sacrifice. God's call to obedience always demands a response. Did you know that when you are obedient others benefit. Not only did Simon benefit from his obedience, but so did his friends in the other boat.

When you obey it lights the way!

1. **When you obey God in the small things, He will allow you to do bigger things.**
2. **When you obey God, it will bless the people that are in your life.**
3. **When you obey God, you will never be disappointed.**

1 John 2:5 (ESV) -

But whoever keeps his word, in him truly the love of God is perfected. By this we may know that we are in him.

STORY //

"When I was a little boy, I would always play outside. When my mom would tell me it was time to come in, I never wanted to. I had a decision to make in that moment. Was I going to be obedient or was I going to be disobedient? There were many times that I chose to disobey. This caused my mom to have to call for me repeatedly and get frustrated at times. I would then receive a punishment for my disobedience. I found that when I would obey my mom and come in on time, it would please her and make her happy. This is true of our relationship with God. When we obey Him, God blesses us and does amazing things with our lives."

> *"Obedience to God is the pathway to the life you really want to live."* - Joyce Meyer [67]

Obedience is hard for a lot of people, because they want to do it their way. God wants us to do it His way. Doing things God's way is the best way. I love what the Bible says in Romans 5:19 (ESV). We are told that, For as by the one man's disobedience the many were made sinners, so by the one man's obedience the many will be made righteous.

When Jesus chose to obey God, you became the beneficiary of God's salvation through a relationship with Him. As you choose to obey God, watch what He will do in your life!

> *"There is no peace in any soul until it is willing to obey the voice of God."* - D. L. Moody [68]

THINK ON IT

Have you seen God's hand on your life as a result of your obedience?

Notes

29

WINNING

DAY 29

WINNING

//BIG THOUGHT//

Winners are not people who never fail, but people who never quit.

In September of 1995, the world-famous Harlem Globetrotters were defeated on the basketball court as they toured Europe with a team made up of former basketball stars. The score was 91-85, and they were defeated in Vienna, Austria. This ended the teams winning streak. The team had won a total of 8,829 straight games since their last defeat in January of 1971. [69]

Some people believe in this philosophy that they are born to lose. As a Christian, a follower of Christ, we have a different take on it. We are born to win!

2 Corinthians 2:14 (ESV) -

But thanks be to God, who in Christ always leads us in triumphal procession...

In this verse, Paul is speaking to the church of Corinth about winning in Christ. God has made you to be a winner. God wants you to win. His desire is that you win in every area of your life.

Ephesians 3:20 (ESV) -

Now to him who is able to do far more abundantly than all that we ask or think, according to the power at work within us.

In order to be a winner, you have to see it, believe it and do it. God believes in you. He sees you and causes you to do great things. The difference between a winner and a loser is that winners train and losers complain. We are winners in Christ Jesus!

The difference in winning and losing is most often not quitting.
– Walt Disney [70]

STORY // Woman with the Issue of Blood
(Mark 5:24-34, ESV)

> "*And he went with Him. And a great crowd followed Him and thronged about Him. And there was a woman who had had a discharge of blood for twelve years, and who had suffered much under many physicians, and had spent all that she had, and was no better but rather grew worse. She had heard the reports about Jesus and came up behind Him in the crowd and touched His garment. For she said, "If I touch even His garments, I will be made well." And immediately the flow of blood dried up, and she felt in her body that she was healed of her disease. And Jesus, perceiving in Himself that power had gone out from Him, immediately turned about in the crowd and said, "Who touched my garments?" And His disciples said to Him, "You see the crowd pressing around you, and yet you say, 'Who touched me?'" And He looked around to see who had done it. But the woman, knowing what had happened to her, came in fear and trembling and fell down before Him and told Him the whole truth. And He said her, "Daughter, your faith has made you well; go in peace, and be healed of your disease.*"

She found a way to win, and Jesus healed her. You were made to win. You are destined to win. God has given you everything that you need to win. God wants you to win at life and has made this possible through Jesus Christ. God's will is for you to succeed. He is for you and not against you. In fact, the Word of God says that His divine power has bestowed on us everything necessary for life and godliness through the rich knowledge of the one who called us by His own glory and excellence. **(2 Peter 1:3)**

Philippians 3:13-14 (ESV) -

Brothers, I do not consider that I have made it my own. But one thing I do: forgetting what lies behind and straining forward to what lies ahead, I press on toward the goal for the prize of the upward call of God in Christ Jesus.

We are destined to win. God made you a winner, a victorious person; you are destined to win. You are unstoppable. You have the seed of greatness in you. He made you to be an achiever, an overcomer in all things!

> *"You were born to win, but to be a winner, you must plan to win, prepare to win, and expect to win."*
> – Zig Ziglar [71]

> *"The victory will go to the one who doesn't quit."*
> – Van Crouch [72]

The Difference Between a Winner and a Loser

A winner says, "I will find a way."	A loser says, "There is no way."
A winner says, "I made a mistake."	A loser says, "I never make mistakes."
A winner goes through the problem.	A loser has no problems.
A winner says, "I'm getting better."	A loser says, "I don't need to improve."
A winner listens to sound counsel.	A loser receives no counsel at all.
A winner respects those in authority.	A loser has no respect to authority.
A winner takes ownership.	A loser casts blame.
A winner says, "I can become better."	A loser sees no need to change.
A winner sees faith.	A loser sees fear.
A winner has self-control.	A loser has no control.

THINK ON IT

Romans 8:37 (ESV) -
"No, in all these things we are more than conquerors through Him who loved us."

You are a conqueror, a winner, and an overcomer!

Notes

Notes

30

POSITIVE

DAY 30

POSITIVE

//BIG THOUGHT//

How you look at things can make a world of difference. Having a positive outlook changes everything.

STORY //

> *"Have you heard the story of the farmer who was discouraged with his farm? So, he decided to sell the land and move somewhere else. He got a realtor to look the farm over and prepare a sales ad, but before putting it in the paper, the realtor called and read the proposed ad to him, saying, "See if this meets with your approval." The ad spoke of a good location, a well-maintained house, sturdy barns, lush pasture lands, a beautiful pond, fertile soil, and a great view. The farmer listened carefully, and then said, "Read that to me again." So, the realtor read it to him again. Finally, the farmer said, "No, don't print that ad. I've changed my mind. I've always wanted a place like that. I'm not going to sell."* – Source Unknown

You see, how you look at something can make a world of difference in how you behave. Do you see the positivity of the life you live in? Or do you only focus on the negative?

The Bible tells you in Philippians 4:8 (ESV) exactly how to think – Finally, brothers, whatever is true, whatever is honorable, whatever is just, whatever is pure, whatever is lovely, whatever is commendable, if there is any excellence, if there is anything worthy of praise, think about these things.

We ought to commit that verse to memory, realizing that what so many are doing today is the exact opposite. Sometimes we focus so much on the negative side of life instead of the positive.

STORY // King Jehoshaphat Goes to War
(2 Chronicles 20:1-25, ESV)

"*After this the Moabites and Ammonites, and with them some of the Meunites, came against Jehoshaphat for battle. Some men came and told Jehoshaphat, "A great multitude is coming against you from Edom, from beyond the sea; and, behold, they are in Hazazon-tamar" (that is, Engedi). Then Jehoshaphat was afraid and set his face to seek the Lord, and proclaimed a fast throughout all Judah. And Judah assembled to seek help from the Lord; from all the cities of Judah they came to seek the Lord. And Jehoshaphat stood in the assembly of Judah and Jerusalem, in the house of the Lord, before the new court, and said, "O Lord, God of our fathers, are you not God in heaven? You rule over all the kingdoms of the nations. In your hand are power and might, so that none is able to withstand you. Did you not, our God, drive out the inhabitants of this land before your people Israel, and give it forever to the descendants of Abraham your friend? And they have lived in it and have built for you in it a sanctuary for your name, saying, 'If disaster comes upon us, the sword, judgment, or pestilence, or famine, we will stand before this house and before you—for your name is in this house—and cry out to you in our affliction, and you will hear and save.' And now behold, the men of Ammon and Moab and Mount Seir, whom you would not let Israel invade when they came from the land of Egypt, and whom they avoided and did not destroy— behold, they reward us by coming to drive us out of your possession, which you have given us to inherit. O our God, will you not execute judgment on them? For we are powerless against this great horde that is coming against us. We do not know what to do, but our eyes are on you." Meanwhile all Judah stood before the Lord, with their little ones, their wives, and their children. And the Spirit of the Lord came upon Jahaziel the son of Zechariah, son of Benaiah, son of Jeiel, son of Mattaniah, a Levite of the sons of Asaph, in the midst of the assembly. And he said, "Listen, all Judah and inhabitants of Jerusalem and King Jehoshaphat: Thus says the Lord to you, 'Do not be afraid and do not be dismayed at this great horde, for the battle is not yours but God's. Tomorrow go down against them. Behold, they will come up by the ascent of Ziz. You will find them at the end of the valley, east of the wilderness of Jeruel. You will not need to fight in this battle. Stand firm, hold your position, and see the salvation of the Lord on your behalf, O Judah and Jerusalem.' Do not be afraid and do not be dismayed. Tomorrow go out against them, and the Lord will be with you." Then Jehoshaphat bowed his head with his face to the ground, and all Judah and the inhabitants of Jerusalem fell down before the Lord, worshipping the Lord. And the Levites, of the Kohathites and the Korahites, stood up to praise the Lord, the God of Israel, with a very loud voice. And they rose early in the morning and went out into the wilderness of Tekoa. And when they went out, Jehoshaphat stood and said, "Hear me, Judah and inhabitants of Jerusalem! Believe in the Lord your God, and you will be established; believe his prophets, and you will succeed." And when he had taken counsel with the people, he appointed those who were to sing to the Lord and praise him in holy attire, as they went before the army, and say, "Give thanks to the Lord, for his steadfast love endures forever." And when they began to sing and praise, the Lord set an ambush against the men of Ammon, Moab, and Mount Seir, who had come against Judah, so that they were routed. For the men of Ammon and Moab rose against the inhabitants of Mount Seir, devoting them to destruction, and when they had made an end of the inhabitants of Seir, they all helped to destroy one another. When Judah came to the watchtower of the wilderness, they looked toward the horde, and behold, there were dead bodies lying on the ground; none had escaped. When Jehoshaphat and his people came to take their spoil, they found among them, in great numbers, goods, clothing, and precious things, which they took for themselves until they could carry no more. They were three days in taking the spoil, it was so much.* ”

Jehoshaphat admitted that there was an issue. He could have easily gone negative and allowed fear to grip his heart. He began to have a self-talk and speak positive. He took responsibility for the words that were coming out of his mouth. He stayed focused on the Lord. When his circumstances seemed impossible, he turned to God and saw God do a miracle and lead them to victory. It is so important to have and keep a positive outlook. You need to keep your eyes focused on the positive side of life. Your positive action combined with positive outlook will always cause you to be successful.

Philippians 2:14-16 talks about doing everything without grumbling, arguing, or pointing fingers. It talks about being positive in life.

//CONFESSION//

I will be positive.
I will talk positive.
I will live positive.
I will walk positive.
I will think positive.
And positive things will happen.

Your mind is a powerful thing. When you fill it with positive thoughts, your life will start to change.

5 Ways to Stay Positive in a Negative World -

1. **Pray**

2. **Read God's Word**

3. **Spend time worshipping the Lord**

4. **Be around positive people**

5. **Have a spirit of gratitude for what you have**

Some practical ways to help you stay positive are –

» Watch the content of the music you listen to
» Be aware of the type of movies you watch
» Keep your self-talk and conversations positive
» Get rid of the secret or destructive habits you have
» Be mindful of the places you go

The Bible tells us to be aware of our thoughts and to take control of them. **(2 Corinthians 10:5 ESV)**

THINK ON IT

Positivity is contagious! Being around positive people will energize you, help you, and encourage you. Choose today to be positive.

"The positive thinker sees the invisible, feels the intangible, and achieves the impossible."
– Winston Churchill [73]

Notes

31

GIVING

DAY 31

GIVING

//BIG THOUGHT//

Giving is living!

STORY // The Queen's Maid

"*Many, many years ago there was a woman who served the Queen as her personal maid. After 50 years of faithful service, the Queen passed away and the maid was dismissed. Before she was dismissed, she received a plaque for her service. However, she had never learned to read and couldn't read the plaque. She was poor and moved to the poor side of town. She settled in a small shanty down by the river.*

One day a reporter came by and through a window saw the plaque hanging on what looked like an abandoned shack. He knocked on the door and to his surprise an elderly woman answered. The reporter asked who she was and where she got that plaque? The woman shared with him how she used to serve the queen. He asked her if she knew what the plaque said. She did not. He told her that the plaque stated that the queen had given her a house on her property with her own servants. It was hers to claim!" – Source Unknown

When you serve and give to others it opens the door for greater opportunities. Most people don't realize the potential that giving can have when you keep your heart right and pure before God. When you serve with a pure heart and unto the Lord, He desires to bless you! The Bible says in Acts 20:35 that you are more blessed when you give then when you receive. Givers always have more than enough. Our natural default is not to give, but it is to be selfish and self-seeking. Think about children, they have to be taught how to share. It doesn't come naturally. The only way to understand true giving is through the Word of God. You must understand what has been given to you from God which is eternal life. Jesus is the greatest gift ever given. Our example to follow is the one that has been laid out before us in the gift of Jesus.

Luke 6:38 (ESV) -

Give, and it will be given to you. Good measure, pressed down, shaken together, running over, will be put into your lap. For with the measure you use it will be measured back to you.

What this verse is saying, is that the measure in which you give will be the measure in which you receive. This verse is not talking about just money, it is talking about every area of your life. Giving is trusting God to take care of you more than you can take care of yourself.

//TAKE A LOOK //

Acts 20:35 (ESV) -

In all things I have shown you that by working hard in this way we must help the weak and remember the words of the Lord Jesus, how he himself said, 'It is more blessed to give than to receive.'"

Galatians 6:7 (ESV) -

Do not be deceived: God is not mocked, for whatever one sows, that will he also reap.

Generous giving increases our:

1. **Happiness**
2. **Physical health**
3. **Purpose in living**
4. **Avoidance of depression**
5. **Interest in personal growth**

Being a giver comes with a great reward. Having a generous spirit is honoring to God.

STORY // The Widow (Luke 21:1-4, ESV)

> *"Jesus looked up and saw the rich putting their gifts into the offering box, and He saw a poor widow put in two small copper coins. And He said, "Truly, I tell you, this poor widow has put in more than all of them. For they all contributed out of their abundance, but she out of her poverty put in all she had to live on."*

In this story, we see a poor widow giving all she had to the Lord. Jesus goes on to explain that she has given more than those who are rich, because she gave out of her need. Sometimes in life, you may feel like you have nothing to give, but all God is asking for is that you remain faithful in giving. Whether you have a lot or a little, be faithful to be generous. Givers, at all levels, have more than enough. Your greatness is not in what you have, but it is in what you give.

> *"No one has ever become poor by giving."*
> - Anne Frank [74]

THINK ON IT

What are the areas in your life that you need to be more generous in? Some examples are - words, actions, gifts, or time.

Notes

Notes

PRAYER OF SALVATION

PRAYER OF SALVATION

Have you ever made Jesus the Lord and Savior of your life?

If you have not, then pray this prayer below and begin a new life in Christ.

"Lord Jesus, I believe You are the Son of God and ask You to come into my heart. Forgive me of all my sins and cleanse me of all unrighteousness. I believe that You took my sins when You died on the cross. I believe You rose again on the third day. I choose to serve You. Be the Lord and Savior of my life. In Jesus Name, Amen."

Romans 10:13 (ESV) – "For everyone who calls on the name of the Lord will be saved."

If you prayed this prayer for the first time, we would like to know. To send an e-mail or share your testimony, visit us at www.thenxtgeneration.com.

APPENDIX

APPENDIX

SOURCES

ALL SCRIPTURES FROM THE ENGLISH STANDARD VERSION

(All citations were cited using - http://www.easybib.com/cite/view)

DAY 1 //

1. "Baby Jessica." Biography.com, A&E Networks Television, 2 Apr. 2014, www.biography.com/people/baby-jessica-17175736.

DAY 2 //

2. "Vince Lombardi Quote." A-Z Quotes, www.azquotes.com/quote/664849.

3. "No Turning Back." SermonSearch, www.sermonsearch.com/sermon-illustrations/914/no-turning-back/.

DAY 3 //

4. www.biography.com/people/jim-carrey-9542079.

DAY 4 //

5. "Forward." Merriam-Webster, Merriam-Webster, www.merriam-webster.com/dictionary/forward.

DAY 5 //

6. "Average Brain Has Up To 50,000 Daily Thoughts And 70% Of Them Are Negative." MessageToEagle.com, 1 Dec. 2017, www.messagetoeagle.com/average-brain-has-up-to-50000-daily-thoughts/. On site Source - Psychology Today

7. "Story: The Elephant Mindset." Story: The Elephant Mindset | Improve Yourself Daily, www.dailytenminutes.com/2012/06/story-elephant-mindset.html.

DAY 6 //

8. "Zig Ziglar Quotes." BrainyQuote, Xplore, www.brainyquote.com/quotes/zig_ziglar_617744.

DAY 7 //

9. "Faith." Merriam-Webster, Merriam-Webster, www.merriam-webster.com/dictionary/faith.

10. "Dwight L. Moody Quote." A-Z Quotes, www.azquotes.com/quote/1339842.

11. "One Prayer Week 2: God Is Able." NW OKC LifeGroup Leaders, 19 June 2009, 4nwleaders.wordpress.com/2009/06/12/one-prayer-week2-god-is-able/.

DAY 8 //

12. "Stabilizing The Leaning Tower Of ..." https://Www.sermoncentral.com, www.sermoncentral.com/illustrations/sermon-illustration-sermoncentral--stories-government-81903.

DAY 9 //

13. "Phobia List - The Ultimate List of Phobias and Fears." FearOf.net, 10 July 2016, www.fearof.net/.

14. PEGGY SENZARINO, Courier Lee News Service. "Little Girl Found Alive after Night Alone in Cornfield." Waterloo Cedar Falls Courier, 5 July 2006, wcfcourier.com/news/regional/little-girl-found-alive-after-night-alone-in-cornfield/article_ce2350b1-c3f8-56b4-b51f-5b0f2c49b6a8.html.

DAY 10 //

15. "'What Fueled The Great Chicago Fire.'" https://Www.sermoncentral.com, www.sermoncentral.com/sermons/what-fueled-the-great-chicago-fire-gerald-roberts-sermon-on-fire-207298?ref=SermonSerps.

16. Zenger, Jack, and Joseph Folkman. "The Ideal Praise-to-Criticism Ratio." Harvard Business Review, 27 June 2017, hbr.org/2013/03/the-ideal-praise-to-criticism.

17. "Horace Quotes." BrainyQuote, Xplore, www.brainyquote.com/quotes/horace_152507.

DAY 11 //

18. Levin, Michael. "Otherwise Indecipherable." Two Frogs in the Cream, 1 Jan. 1970, otherwiseindecipherable.blogspot.com/2009/08/frogs-in-cream.html.

19. Norman, P. "The Whole World Stinks." Positivity Post, 26 Jan. 2018, positivitypost.com/the-whole-world-stinks/.

20. "Zig Ziglar Quotes." BrainyQuote, Xplore, www.brainyquote.com/quotes/zig_ziglar_381975.

21. "Winston Churchill Quotes." BrainyQuote, Xplore, www.brainyquote.com/quotes/winston_churchill_104164.

DAY 12 //

22. "John C. Maxwell Quote." A-Z Quotes, www.azquotes.com/quote/556482.

23. "A Quote by Albert Camus." Quote by Albert Camus: "Life Is a Sum of All Your Choices". So, What ...", www.goodreads.com/quotes/405686-life-is-a-sum-of-all-your-choices-so-what.

24. "Can't Make Decisions." SermonSearch, www.sermonsearch.com/sermon-illustrations/1478/cant-make-decisions/.

25. "Catherine Pulsifer Quotes." Art Quotes Categories, www.art-quotes.com/auth_search.php?authid=955#.WpsRmmaZPfY.

26. Hall, Dr. Kathleen. "Alter Your Life." Google Books, books.google.com/books?id=Kus5RUf1Ok8C&pg=PA26&lpg=PA26&dq=In%2Bevery%2Bsingle%2Bthing%2C%2Byou%2Bdo%2C%2Byou%2Bare%2Bchoosing%2Ba%2Bdirection.%2BYour%2Blife%2Bis%2Ba%2Bproduct%2Bof%2Bchoices.%2Bkathleen%2Bhall&source=bl&ots=VFXkb5uKV&sig=1scxnomUawa4cbRw6fwiGtWioCM&hl=en&sa=X&ved=0ahUKEwipkeyEi9HZAhVDX60KHVkfDvIQ6AEIMzAC#v=onepage&q=In%20every%20single%20thing%2C%20you%20do%2C%20you%20are%20choosing%20a%20direction.%20Your%20life%20is%20a%20product%20of%20choices.%20kathleen%20hall&f=false.

27. Quote Investigator, quoteinvestigator.com/2011/08/05/lion-gazelle/.

DAY 13 //

28. “Newt Gingrich Quotes.” BrainyQuote, Xplore, www.brainyquote.com/quotes/newt_gingrich_107062.

29. “Perseverance.” Merriam-Webster, Merriam-Webster, www.merriam-webster.com/dictionary/perseverance.

30. “Henry Ford.” Bible.org, bible.org/node/13258.

31. “Charles Spurgeon Quotes.” BrainyQuote, Xplore, www.brainyquote.com/quotes/charles_spurgeon_143068.

DAY 15 //

32. “John C. Maxwell Quotes.” BrainyQuote, Xplore, www.brainyquote.com/quotes/john_c_maxwell_383606.

33. “Praise - Get the Hell Out!” Google Books, books.google.com/books?id=hhVdDQAAQBAJ&pg=PT113&lp-g=PT113&dq=geese%2Bencourage%2Bone%2Banother%2Bto%2Bkeep-%2Bgoing&source=bl&ots=je4YTcI-nE&sig=ZiGFTRRn5RCI15PklGin3P-kMLec&hl=en&sa=X&ved=0ahUKEwju5v2Go9HZAhUKZKwKHfOAC8E-Q6AEIPTAD#v=onepage&q=geese%20encourage%20one%20another%20to%20keep%20going&f=false.

34. “Sermon - So You Will Never Forget.” LifeWay, www.lifeway.com/en/articles/sermon-communion-lords-sup-per-cup-bread-1-corinthians-11.

DAY 16 //

35. “Maya Angelou Quotes.” BrainyQuote, Xplore, www.brainyquote.com/quotes/maya_angelou_634520.

36. “In the Name of Jesus Stop! Telemachus' Story.” Jesseleeproject.com, 8 Aug. 2011, jesseleeproject.com/2010/01/31/in-the-name-of-jesus-stop-telema-chus-story/.

37. “A Quote by Elsie De Wolfe.” Quote by Elsie De Wolfe: "I Am Going to Make

Everything around Me Beautif...", www.goodreads.com/quotes/51441-i-am-going-to-make-everything-around-me-beautiful--.

DAY 17 //

38. "A Policeman Pulls Over 5 Old Ladies For Driving Too Slow And Their Explanation Is Hilarious." Reshareworthy, 15 Oct. 2017, www.reshareworthy.com/speeding-old-ladies-joke/.

DAY 18 //

39. "John C. Maxwell Quote: 'Leader's Potential Is Determined by Those Closest to Him."." John C. Maxwell Quote: Quotefancy, quotefancy.com/quote/841786/John-C-Maxwell-Leader-s-potential-is-determined-by-those-closest-to-him.

40. "A Quote by Jim Rohn." Quote by Jim Rohn: "You Are the Average of the Five People You Spen...", www.goodreads.com/quotes/1798-you-are-the-average-of-the-five-people-you-spend.

41. www.linkedin.com/pulse/story-behind-picture-praying-hands-sons-of-issachar-concepts.

DAY 19 //

42. Ronca, Debra. "How Lion Taming Works." HowStuffWorks, HowStuffWorks, 16 Mar. 2009, entertainment.howstuffworks.com/arts/circus-arts/lion-taming2.htm.

43. "Bruce Lee Quote: 'The Successful Warrior Is the Average Man, with Laser-like Focus."." Bruce Lee Quote: "The Successful Warrior Is the Average Man, with Laser-like Focus." (27 Wallpapers) - Quotefancy, quotefancy.com/quote/78922/Bruce-Lee-The-successful-warrior-is-the-average-man-with-laser-like-focus.

44. "Les Brown Quotes." BrainyQuote, Xplore, www.brainyquote.com/quotes/les_brown_379155.

DAY 20 //

45. "Billy Graham Quotes." BrainyQuote, Xplore,

www.brainyquote.com/quotes/billy_graham_382920.

46. Jelani Faraja. Rethink the Journey: "Reigniting the Spiritual Fire" (The Sincere Church). Kingdom Book and Gift Publishers and Booksellers, 2017.

DAY 21 //

47. Unknown. The Story of a Son - Who Will Take the Son?, www.jaredstory.com/story_of_a_son.html.

DAY 22 //

48. "Thomas A. Edison Quotes." BrainyQuote, Xplore, www.brainyquote.com/quotes/thomas_a_edison_104931.

DAY 23 //

49. quotefancy.com/quote/980718/Bell-Hooks-People-with-healthy-self-esteem-do-not-need-to-create-pretend-identities.

50. "Identity." Merriam-Webster, Merriam-Webster, www.merriam-webster.com/dictionary/identity.

51. "Understanding Your Fingerprint Determines the Significance of Your Imprint." Keith Craft, keithcraft.org/understanding-your-fingerprint-determines-the-significance-of-your-imprint/.

52. "Zig Ziglar Quotes." BrainyQuote, Xplore, www.brainyquote.com/quotes/zig_ziglar_724588.

53. Furtick, Steven. "God Can't Bless Who You Pretend to Be. (See Luke 9:25) https://T.co/rpZZHxA8Glhttps://T.co/UoFEVrpFsr." Twitter, Twitter, 16 Jan. 2016, twitter.com/stevenfurtick/status/688445659741990912?lang=en.

DAY 24 //

54. "Trust." Merriam-Webster, Merriam-Webster, www.merriam-webster.com/dictionary/trust.

55. "MY STORY." Bethany Hamilton - Bethany's Story, soulsurfer.com/story.html.

DAY 25 //

56. “Ferdinand Foch.” Ferdinand Foch - Wikiquote, en.wikiquote.org/wiki/Ferdinand_Foch.

57. https://quoteinvestigator.com/2014/11/21/adventure/

58. “Georg Wilhelm Friedrich Hegel Quotes.” BrainyQuote, Xplore, www.brainyquote.com/quotes/georg_wilhelm_friedrich_h_101479.

59. Pringle, Phil; Twitter, 10 June 2015, twitter.com/philpringle/status/608763140222894080.

60. https://bible.org/illustration/truth-or-fiction

DAY 26 //

61. “Last Stand.” SermonSearch, www.sermonsearch.com/sermon-illustrations/1183/last-stand/.

62. Einstein, Albert. “Albert Einstein Quote: ‘A Ship Is Always Safe at the Shore, but That Is Not What It Is Built for.".” Albert Einstein Quote: "A Ship Is Always Safe at the Shore, but That Is Not What It Is Built for." (24 Wallpapers) - Quotefancy, quotefancy.com/quote/6051/Albert-Einstein-A-ship-is-always-safe-at-the-shore-but-that-is-not-what-it-is-built-for.

DAY 27 //

63. “Mother Teresa Quote: Quotefancy, quotefancy.com/quote/869269/Mother-Teresa-It-s-not-about-how-much-you-do-but-how-much-love-you-put-in-to-what-you-do.

64. “Love.” Merriam-Webster, Merriam-Webster, www.merriam-webster.com/dictionary/love.

65. “The True and Tragic Story of John Griffith and the Memphis Express.” The True and Tragic Story of John Griffith and the Memphis Express. - Part One - Wattpad, www.wattpad.com/46594727-the-true-and-tragic-story-of-john-griffith-and-the.

DAY 28 //

66. "Edwin Louis Cole Quotes." BrainyQuote, Xplore, www.brainyquote.com/quotes/edwin_louis_cole_360107.

67. "Joyce Meyer Quotes." BrainyQuote, Xplore, www.brainyquote.com/quotes/joyce_meyer_565161.

68. "Dwight L. Moody Quote." A-Z Quotes, www.azquotes.com/quote/1412296.

DAY 29 //

69. "Defeated the Harlem Globetrotters." Bible.org, bible.org/illustration/defeated-harlem-globetrotters.

70. www.azquotes.com/quote/487359. (Walt Disney)

71. "Zig Ziglar Quotes." BrainyQuote, Xplore, www.brainyquote.com/quotes/zig_ziglar_381983.

72. "The Will To Win." https://Www.sermoncentral.com, www.sermoncentral.com/sermons/the-will-to-win-rob-yanok-sermon-on-power-126702.

DAY 30 //

73. "Winston Churchill Quote: (24 Wallpapers) - Quotefancy, quotefancy.com/quote/758984/Winston-Churchill-The-positive-thinker-sees-the-invisible-feels-the-intangible-and.

DAY 31 //

74. "Anne Frank Quotes." BrainyQuote, Xplore, www.brainyquote.com/quotes/anne_frank_379577

ADDITIONAL REFERENCES –

- "Fear Of The Unknown." Zechariah Newman, 21 Oct. 2014, zechariahnewman.com/2014/10/21/fear-of-the-unknown/.

- "There Will Be No Peace." SermonQuotes, 8 Nov. 2016, sermonquotes.com/authors/9643-will-no-peace.html.

- www.gracequotes.org, gracequotes.org/?topic=preaching-effectiveness&author-quote=g-campbell-morgan&s=preaching.

- Jentezen Franklin, www.jentezenfranklin.org/daily-devotions/two-questions.

- "Rethink the Journey-'Reigniting the Spiritual Fire.'" Google Books, books.google.com/books?id=AC8qDwAAQBAJ&pg=PA85&lpg=PA85&dq=man%2Bwho%2Bworked%2Bas%2Ba%2Bmessenger%2Bin%2Ba%2Bphoto%2Blab&source=bl&ots=X1JpBosqSl&sig=9Y0DFtRM348B8E1yvIpwZ8K-jds&hl=en&sa=X&ved=0ahUKEwi1l by6M7ZAhVKVK0KHUgYAK0Q6AEIKTAA#v=onepage&q=man%20who%20worked%20as%20a%20messenger%20in%20a%20photo%20lab&f=false.

- Tasler, Nick. "What Is Your Momentum Factor?" Psychology Today, Sussex Publishers, 30 Aug. 2012, www.psychologytoday.com/blog/strategic-thinking/201208/what-is-your-momentum-factor.

- www.brainyquote.com/topics/quit.